Tying Contemporary
SALTWATER FLIES

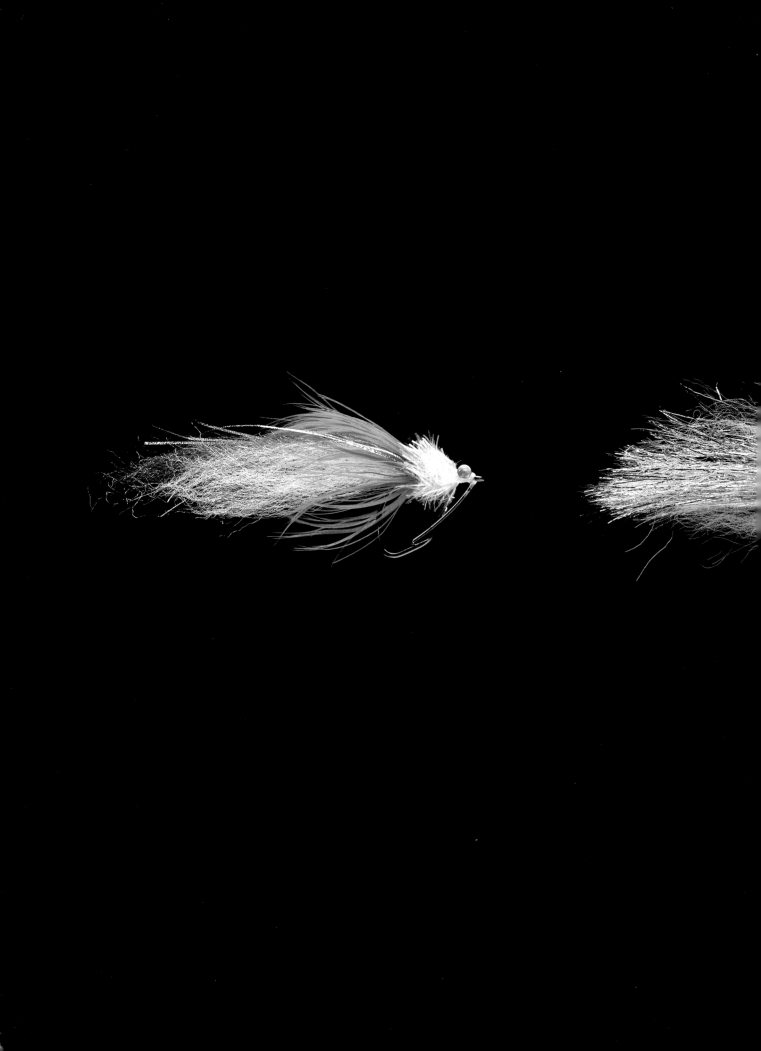

Tying Contemporary
SALTWATER FLIES
AN ILLUSTRATED STEP-BY-STEP GUIDE

by david klausmeyer

· ORIGINAL ARTWORK BY LARRY LARGAY ·

THE COUNTRYMAN PRESS
WOODSTOCK, VERMONT

Library of Congress Cataloging-in-Publication Data
Klausmeyer, David, 1958–
   Tying contemporary saltwater flies : an illustrated step-by-step guide /
David Klausmeyer ; original artwork by Larry Largay.—1st ed.
     p. cm.;
   Includes bibliographical references (p. 145).
   ISBN 0-88150-524-2
   1. Fly tying. 2. Flies, Artificial—Pictorial works. 3. Saltwater fly fishing. I. Title.
SH451.K53 2002
688.7'9124—dc21
                                                                      2002067430

All photographs accompanying the tying instructions and fly patterns
by David Klausmeyer
All original artwork, chapter opening photographs, other artistic photographs
by Larry Largay
Cover and interior designs by Larry Largay

Published by THE COUNTRYMAN PRESS, P.O. Box 748,
Woodstock, Vermont 05091
Distributed by W.W. NORTON & COMPANY, 500 Fifth Avenue, New York, NY 10110

Printed in Spain

10 9 8 7 6 5 4 3 2 1

acknowledgments

Throughout this book you'll find flies and patterns submitted by guides
and a few other very talented tiers. All of these folks spend a lot of
time on the water, and their flies are worth tying and using. Some of their
names you will know, some you won't. One of my goals was to include
a selection of flies from tiers whose work has never appeared in print.
Thanks to all of the tiers for their time, friendship and support.

Many other people have helped to make
this book possible.

First, there's my good friend and colleague,
Larry Largay. Larry is the finest angling
illustrator in the business. He has provided
all of the artwork, artistic photography, as
well as the design concept for this book.
Larry is defining how books will be written,
illustrated, designed, and produced in the
future.

My good friends at *Fly Tyer, American
Angler,* and *Saltwater Fly Fishing* magazines
are always a wealth of ideas and inspiration.

Several manufacturers have given critical
support to this project. I'd like to extend
my thanks to Wapsi Fly, Umpqua Feather
Merchants, Whiting Farms, Dyna-King,
and Abel Products.

I must also thank my family for their support. My wife says I get crabby when I have
a deadline, and writers and editors have
lots of deadlines.

The good folks at The Countryman Press
have also been very kind and supportive.
They have given Larry Largay and me free
hand to write, take pictures, and design this
book. Kermit Hummel, the publisher at The
Countryman Press, understands the future
of publishing.

And like my first book, future books, and all of my magazine articles,
this volume is dedicated to the anonymous gentleman at a sporting-goods store
in Oklahoma who first showed me how to tie a fly. I was just
a kid—growing up far from saltwater fishing—and he showed me how
to make a bass bug. Little did he know the seed that was planted.

contents

Introduction **1**

CHAPTER **1** **Materials & Tools** **2**

CHAPTER **2** **Basic Flies** **11**

CHAPTER **3** **Small Baitfish** **33**

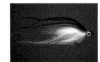

CHAPTER **4** **Tarpon Flies** **63**

CHAPTER **5** **Shrimp, Squid, & Eels** **79**

CHAPTER **6** **Flats Flies That Catch Fish** **109**

CHAPTER **7** **Tricks with Epoxy & Silicone** **133**

Appendix **145**

Index **149**

introduction

For the past several years I have demonstrated fly tying at the International Fly Tying Symposium, a great angling and fly-tying event held in New Jersey. A couple of years ago, Barry Serviente, the proprietor of The Anglers Art, was setting up a large display of books at the symposium. The Anglers Art is one of the biggest retailers of fly-fishing books in the world. Whether new or antique, if it's a book about fly fishing, Barry has it or can get it for you.

Barry and I exchanged greetings and started chatting about the large number of fly-fishing books on the market. We both agreed that if these books, as well as magazines and instructional videos, had been around when we began our angling careers, we would have spent a lot less time going through trial-and-error, and a lot more time actually catching fish. It then occurred to me to ask him a question: what book hasn't been written?

"A book about tying saltwater flies," he quickly replied.

"You've got to be kidding," I said. "There are already several books about saltwater flies."

Barry agreed that there are books about saltwater flies, and most are excellent and worth reading (you'll find several listed in the bibliography at the end of this volume). He pointed out, however, that those books are about saltwater flies and how to fish them—not how to tie them.

"I get calls from customers wanting a book about how to tie saltwater patterns, and I really have nothing to offer them," Barry continued. "That's the book you should write."

Throughout this book you'll find fly patterns submitted by guides and a few other very talented tiers. All of these folks spend a lot of time on the water, and their flies are worth tying and using. Some of their names you will know, some you won't. One of my goals was include a selection of good tiers whose flies have never appeared in print. I did contact a few other tiers who did not respond to my letters, but I didn't contact every saltwater guide or fly tier; time and space was limited. And just because someone's flies do not appear in this book does not mean his flies or guiding services are not worthy; there are a lot of great guides and tiers I wish I could have included. Maybe next time. I would like to thank all of the fellows who did provide flies for their time, friendship, and support.

I should mention something about these patterns. Some of the guides and tiers sent their flies accompanied with complete written descriptions including the full recipes of materials and how to fish the fly; others submitted information that wasn't so precise. When a guide or tier did not provide a recipe, I prepared the pattern as faithfully as I could. In a few patterns, I have also suggested substitute materials for hard-to-find ingredients. You'll also notice in some patterns that specific hooks are recommended, and in others they are not. When a guide or tier listed a hook, I included it in the recipe; when they did not, I only offer a general description.

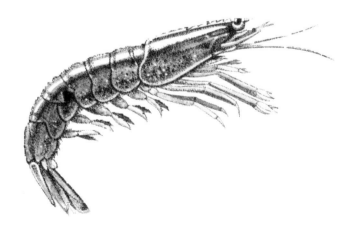

chapter 1

WHAT YOU'LL NEED TO TIE GREAT SALTWATER FLIES

Just as with tying freshwater flies, the first patterns created to catch saltwater gamefish where made with thread, feathers, fur, and maybe a little tinsel. Those simple flies caught plenty of fish. In recent years, there has been an explosion in the variety of new fly-tying materials; the wall of your local fly shop probably glitters like a Christmas tree from all of the bright synthetic materials hanging on the peg boards. Rayon, nylon, plastics, polypropylene, Mylar, and all manner of goo's and gunks have revolutionized how we think about flies and fly tying. Some of these materials were invented specifically for crafting flies; many were appropriated from other industries and adapted to fly tying. Whatever the case, we now have at our disposal a huge variety of ingredients with which to tie flies, and additional materials are being marketed every year. We've come a very long way from using simply feathers and fur.

What makes a good fly-tying material? The answer depends upon who you ask. Tom Schmuecker, the head honcho at Wapsi Fly, Inc., the world's largest distributor of fly-tying materials, once told me that for a material to be successful, fly tiers have to see the value of the ingredient when it is hanging on the fly-shop wall. He used Flashabou, the popular glittery tinsel, as an example. Tom said that tiers could easily see how to incorporate Flashabou into their flies; they didn't have to be told how to use it. EZ Body and Corsair tubing, which we will use to tie the bodies on some flies in the following chapters, are other examples of materials that sell themselves. But Tom is in the business of selling feathers, furs, and glittery stuff to people like us; he likes a material that sells itself.

I think if we dig a little deeper into Tom's reply, we'll find some good answers that will guide us when determining which materials to buy. First and foremost, a material should be fairly easy to use. There's little joy in having to struggle with a material to get it to stay in place or take the shape you wish. A good material should also be durable, especially when you are casting to toothy saltwater fish. Hopefully the material comes in a range of colors or can be colored with permanent markers or paints so you can use it to tie a variety of flies. All of this, of course, might seems a little obvious. Here's a better question: what materials should you buy?

This is an especially tough question for new tiers. I've taught a lot of fly-tying classes, and I always have students show up with boxes of useless stuff they've never used. With so many materials on the market, where do you begin? The best plan is to select a limited number of flies—perhaps three or four—that you'll need for the type of fishing you plan to do. Look through the pattern recipes in this book; you'll find flies for catching all of the popular saltwater gamefish. Acquire the materials necessary to tie only those flies. Often times you'll be able to use the same hooks to tie two or three different patterns; that's an immediate savings for your wallet. You'll also find that some other materials can be used to tie different flies. Become an expert at tying those few patterns and have fun using them to catch fish. Add new patterns to your fly-tying repertoire as your talents increase. Buy new materials gradually and you'll be more satisfied with your tying and have a collection of materials that you'll really use.

You'll only need a few tools for tying saltwater flies. Here again there is a lot from which to choose, but there's no need for confusion. I'll make a few recommendations that will cover most price ranges, but you should also get input from other tiers. Plan to spend a few bucks and acquire the best tools you can; remember that most of the tools are a lifetime investment, and hopefully you'll spend many enjoyable hours using them.

There's no way I can include a review of all of the available fly-tying tools and materials. Even if I tried, something new would come on the market before this book reaches your hands. My goal is to give you a good grounding in the selection of quality tools and materials.

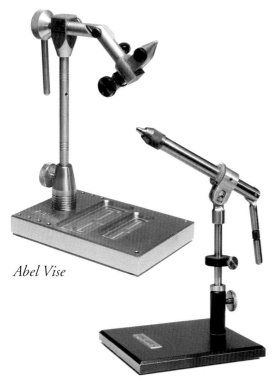

Abel Vise

Dyna-King Vise

THE TOOLS OF THE TRADE

The Vise

I know how frustrating it can be to take up a new hobby: you get all kinds of recommendations that seem to be designed to separate you from your money. Fly tying is no different; we're awash in gadgets, and it's hard to distinguish those that will really help you tie a better fly from those that will only take up space on your tying table. Choosing the best vise for tying saltwater flies should be easy, but it's not. Here are a few tips for selecting a vise for creating saltwater patterns.

First, the vise must hold a large hook securely; it's frustrating to have the hook slip up and down while tying the fly. While this seems pretty obvious, I take this point a step further: a quality vise will hold a large hook securely without the tier having to place undue force on the jaw locking mechanism. This is an important point. I've auditioned a couple of vises that are beautifully machined from the finest materials, but they required a lot of adjustment and quite a bit of pressure on the locking levers used to close the jaws and grasp the hook; so much pressure, in fact, that I thought something on the vise might eventually fatigue and break. The best vise will clamp a hook with the tier having to place only a moderate amount of pressure on the locking mechanism.

A good vise for tying saltwater flies also provides ample working room all around the hook. This seems like a simple point, but some vises are so overbuilt that it's difficult to easily get at the hook to tie the fly. With respect to having access to the hook, a vise that rotates will allow you to turn the hook over in the vise to examine the other side of the fly in between tying steps—a very nice feature.

It's your call when choosing between a pedestal-model vise or one that grasps the edge of the tying table with a C-clamp. Some tiers like C-clamp vises because they can apply extra tension to the thread and these vises—and thus the hooks—remain stationary. Of course, a C-clamp vise limits you to working only at your tying bench and other tables that accommodate the clamp. I like a pedestal vise because it gives me freedom to work wherever I wish: the tying bench, classrooms, hotel rooms, or on a lapboard while sitting in my easy chair—my favorite place to tie.

Finally, you must select a vise that will accommodate the range of hook sizes you plan to use. Almost all manufacturers offer vises they say will work with the full range of fly-tying hooks. Some of these vises perform as advertised—some don't do it so well. I have one premium vise—you'd probably know the name if I mentioned it—that meets all of my criteria: it holds hooks securely, the hooks are very accessible, and the jaws of the newer models rotate. This vise is also one of the simplest to use: squeeze a lever, insert the hook between the jaws, and then release the lever. This vise is American made and is "premium" in every sense of the word. The manufacturer advertises that it works with something like hook sizes 28 to 4/0, so you can tie small freshwater midges to large saltwater flies with the same vise. A couple of years ago, after spending most of the summer dressing large saltwater flies, I noticed that small dry-fly hooks were slipping up and down in the jaws. It turned out that one of the jaws had fatigued and bent outward. The manufacturer was very nice and replaced the jaws free of charge (he returned the repaired vise to me in less than a week). I still consider it one of the finest vises on the market, but I save it for tying freshwater flies; I stopped using this old workhorse for tying saltwater patterns.

Some manufacturers offer vises with interchangeable jaws of different sizes, allowing you to match the jaws to the size of the flies you're tying: small jaws for dressing tiny freshwater patterns, medium-sized jaws that accommodate most freshwater and smaller saltwater hooks, and large jaws for clamping big saltwater irons. While some manufacturers do offer vises that actually work with the full range of hook sizes, these versatile, multi-jaw vises will give you the ability to work with any tying hook on the market.

Finally, some companies manufacture vises specifically designed for tying saltwater flies. Saltwater fly-tying vises come with heavier jaws, and usually offer extra working room around hooks. These premium vises are perfect for tying saltwater flies, but it's tough to tie small freshwater flies in their beefier jaws.

Let me say a word about the cost of fly-tying vises. First, I hope you already own a vise that will work for tying the flies in this book; rather than buying tools, you'll be able to spend your money on materials and start tying. If you do need a vise, purchase the best you can comfortably afford. There are some very good vises that cost less than a hundred dollars; the D.H. Thompson Model A and Griffin Enterprises Patriot vises are affordable industry standards.

At the other end of the spectrum, the Dyna-King Saltwater Special, which I am using in the fly-tying photographs throughout this book, is a wonderful specialized saltwater fly-tying vise: the jaws are heavy-duty, there is ample room to work around the hook, and it requires very little pressure to close the lever and tightly grasp the hook. This is a terrific vise that will last a lifetime. If you're an avid saltwater angler, then you're already familiar with Abel reels. Abel also makes a lovely vise. Like everything Steve Abel offers, this vise is first-rate: fine machining, beautiful finish, and built to last. Yes, these vises, as well as the popular vises offered by Renzetti, Inc., are not inexpensive, but they are lifetime investments. If you become a serious fly tier, you'll probably spend more time using your vise than you will a comparably priced rod or reel. If cost isn't a major consideration, invest in one of these fine vises.

Scissors

Purchase a set of cheap scissors for cutting wire, tinsel, monofilament, and other hard materials. When they become dull, toss them out and get a new set. Most shops carry cheap, imported scissors that cost a couple of bucks.

You'll also want a high-quality pair of scissors that maintain sharp blades. The blades on better scissors, such as those offered by the Dr. Slick company, also don't come loose from each other and make a cleaner cut. Use these scissors for cutting thread and other soft materials, and for clipping and trimming materials behind the hook eye before completing the thread head of the fly. To facilitate close, delicate work, these scissors should have fine points.

If you have two identical pair of scissors—one for cutting hard materials, the other for delicate work—place a piece of masking tape around the handle of one pair. Use this set of scissors for cutting only hard or soft materials.

OTHER FLY-TYING TOOLS YOU'LL NEED

Much to the chagrin of the fly-tying tool manufacturers, I'm a minimalist. After a good vise and pair of scissors, there's not much else on my tying bench.

I do have three or four bobbins. A bobbin holds the thread while you tie. A bobbin performs two important functions (there might be more, but these are what matter to me). First, it provides tension on the thread while you work; you can even allow the thread to hang from the hook while you prepare additional materials. Second, since you hold the bobbin and not the thread (you grasp the bobbin with the spool cradled in your palm), the thread remains cleaner.

Avoid cheap bobbins; the ends of the tubes often have microscopic burrs that will nick and fray the thread. The best bobbins have ceramic inserts to eliminate the possibility of these burrs. A ceramic-insert bobbin costs only a few dollars, and like a quality vise, it is a lifetime investment. It's worth the extra couple of dollars to purchase a good bobbin.

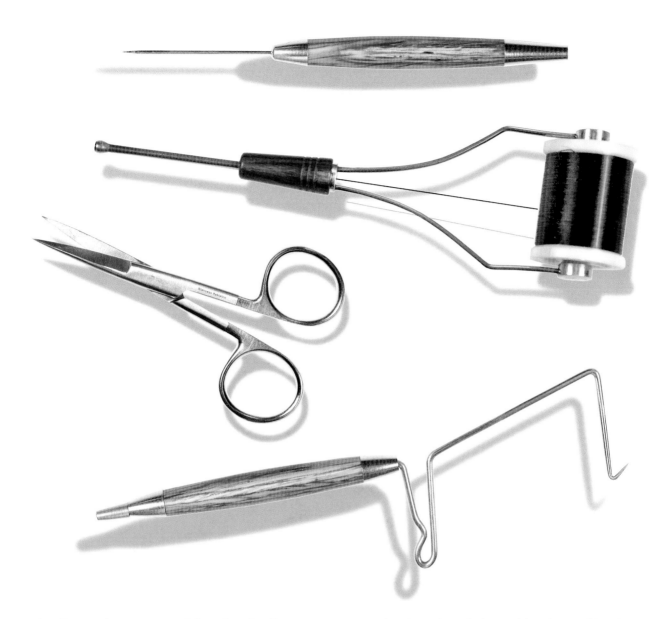

A bodkin is also a very useful tool. A bodkin is nothing more than a large needle inserted into some sort of handle: wood, metal, a piece of antler, or some other material. A bodkin is great for separating strands of material, mixing epoxy, cleaning head cement from a hook eye, and numerous other odd jobs.

Some tiers like whip-finishers (a whip-finish is the knot used to tie off the thread when completing a fly). I once learned to use a whip-finisher—as an author and editor of fly-tying books and magazines, I felt sort of obligated to try—but then I tossed it aside. It was just one more thing to clutter my tying bench. I usually tie off the thread with three or four half-hitches, which I apply with my fingers (I can also make a whip-finish using only my fingers—it's sort of a neat trick for tying demonstrations), clip

the thread, and then add a drop of head cement or epoxy. Use a whip-finisher if you like; besides being a nifty tool, you'll also amaze people who have never mastered it.

Besides a vise and bobbin, I don't think I could tie flies without a supply of single-edged razor blades. While I use scissors to cut materials to length, I do almost all of my other cutting and trimming with razor blades. Nothing is as sharp, or as cheap, as a razor blade. When a blade dulls, just pitch it and get another.

There are a few other tools you'll need to create specific types of saltwater flies. Most of these are used to make flies with epoxy and other glues. Let's save our discussion of these specialized tools for the appropriate chapters.

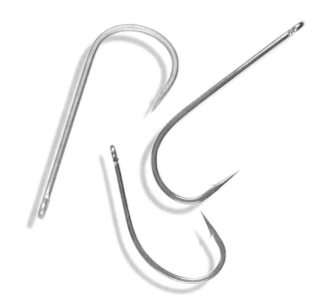

MATERIALS

Hooks

Someone once said the hook is the chassis of the fly; I don't remember who. So let's start here: with the chassis.

While you might be able to get away with using a slightly "cheap" hook when fishing for many freshwater species—especially smaller fish—you should use the best hooks you can afford when tying saltwater flies. There are several obvious reasons.

First, the best hooks are properly tempered and maintain a very sharp point. This is extremely important because many saltwater species have very hard mouths. Tarpon are an excellent example; the interior of their mouths are like steel plates, and the hook point must be needle sharp if it is to sink home. Properly tempered hooks are also strong and resist bending or breaking during a prolonged fight with a big trophy fish.

Second, the best hooks are made of stainless steel—an expensive material—and so resist corroding. Nothing is worse than tying a box full of flies, only to have them rust as the season progresses. A couple of manufacturers offer very nice hooks that are coated with tin. These hooks are designed for saltwater fishing, and they do resist corroding—as long as the tin is not removed. Most good saltwater anglers carry hook hones; guides especially are always sharpening and fiddling with the points on their clients' hooks.

When you sharpen the point of a plated hook, you remove the tin and expose the wire to the salt. Put that sharpened fly away after fishing, and the point will rust. Plated hooks aren't necessarily cheap, so spend the couple of extra bucks to upgrade to real stainless-steel hooks.

Today, freshwater fly tiers have a smorgasbord of hooks in different sizes and shapes; saltwater tiers have a more limited selection. When tying many freshwater patterns, the hooks create the basic shape of the fly; bent-shank nymph and scud hooks are good examples. With saltwater patterns, the hook is usually just the place to tie on the materials; the shank plays very little role in creating the shape of the fly. As a result, most saltwater hooks have straight shanks. Exceptions to this rule are specialized hooks such as the bent-shank Tiemco TMC411S, which are used to tie the Bend-Back series of flies, or the Mustad CK74S SS kinked-shank hooks which are used for constructing poppers.

Saltwater hooks also come in a narrower range of sizes. While there are no mandated industry standards for measuring hook size—which is generally accepted to mean the width of the gap—most manufacturers seem to use comparable size specifications; the sizes of Mustad, Daiichi, Dai-Ricci and a couple of other companies seem to be similar. One notable exception are the hooks manufactured by Varivas; these all have wide gaps to increase hook-ups.

Circle hooks are a unique departure from regularly shaped saltwater hooks. These unusual hooks are receiving a lot of attention among conservation-minded anglers interested in practicing catch-and-release.

Circle hooks, which are bent so that the point faces the shank, look as though they wouldn't catch a thing including your thumb. But don't let their improbable shape fool you. Circle hooks were first used in the commercial tuna-fishing industry, and some captains realized an 85 percent increase in their hook-up rates, something that should get the attention of sport anglers. The first sport-fishing use of circle hooks was for halibut in the Pacific Northwest. On my trips to the Florida Keys, however, I'm seeing an increasing number of guides, especially those specializing in catching big tarpon, using flies tied on circle hooks. A day of guided fishing isn't cheap, and many guides thrive on repeat business; they wouldn't dare hand clients flies tied a hooks in which they didn't have complete confidence.

A circle hook works like this. As soon as the jaws of the fish begin to close around the fly, the hook rotates in the direction of point penetration. The hook-set is accomplished through pressure, not by forcefully setting the hook. As the hook rotates in the fish's mouth, the line tightens and the hook point penetrates the lip, usually in the corner of the mouth. A fish caught on a circle hook will find it almost impossible to throw that hook. Unlike a regular J-shaped hook, a circle hook doesn't back straight out; it must be rotated to be removed.

Eagle Claw is the leader in developing circle hooks, and that company offers fly circle hooks in several sizes. I wish every saltwater tier would experiment with these new hooks. You might not want to take a box full of flies dressed on circle hooks on your dream trip to the Fiji Islands; a once-in-a-lifetime adventure is a poor place to experiment with new tackle. But tie a few patterns on circle hooks for the fishing you do the most; compare circle hooks with those you usually use and see if they have a place in your fishing.

Thread

I suspect more tiers give less consideration to the thread they use than just about any material. That's a shame because thread is just about the most important material on your tying bench: it's the thing used to actually tie the fly (hence the term "fly tying") and holds the whole thing together. The correct thread can make it easier to tie a fly, it contributes to the final appearance of the fly, and it enhances the durability of the finished product.

Having made my pitch for the importance of thread, it might seem strange to say that I keep only a few spools in my saltwater tying kit. In fact, I do most of my tying using only two or three different spools. First, let's talk about colors.

While black thread is important for tying saltwater flies, white is also commonly used. The reason is simple: most saltwater flies are tied using white, yellow, and other light-colored materials. When these flies get wet, black thread can have a tendency to show through and spoil the appearance of the fly; white thread, on the other hand, can become slightly translucent and blend into the materials. White thread can also be tied on the hook and colored with permanent markers. Chartreuse thread is also important because so many patterns are crafted with chartreuse-colored materials. There are a few patterns that call for brown, olive, yellow, a couple of other colors, but you'll use black, white, and chartreuse thread more than any of the others.

On the other hand, why use colored thread at all? Have you tried any of the clear monofilament threads? If you haven't, then pick up a couple of spools and give it go. Monofilament thread comes in several sizes, some of which are perfect for tying saltwater flies. Clear monofilament thread will never spoil the appearance of a wet fly, and allows the colors of the underlying materials to show through the finished head of the fly. You will have to pay a little more attention to how you layer the materials on the hook—you won't be able to use an opaque colored thread to "neaten up" the head of the fly—but you will be able to create flies that have a nice, even coloration from their noses to their tails. Monofilament thread is also an essential ingredient for crafting epoxy flies.

In addition to the limited number of colors of thread you'll need, saltwater tying also requires only a couple of sizes of thread. Sizes 3/0 and A are general all-purpose sizes. For the bigger patterns, some tiers like Gudebrod size G.

Hackle

Rather than discuss all of the different feathers you'll find throughout the book, I'd like to limit this discussion to selecting saddle hackle. There are so many hackle products on the market that it's easy to select the wrong feathers for the flies you tie. Let's talk about the saddle hackle feathers you'll need to tie saltwater flies.

The first type of saddle hackle has a rounded, rather full appearance. These feathers are used to tie a wide variety of baitfish imitations and classic tarpon patterns, and come in a rainbow of colors. I suggest asking for "strung" saddle hackle at the local fly shop; these feathers usually have this nice full shape. This type of hackle can also be purchased "on the skin," and is often referred to as streamer hackle. Purchasing an entire skin of hackle, which often costs only a couple of dollars more than strung hackle, will give you feathers in a wide variety of sizes.

The second type of saddle hackle is long and skinny. These feathers come from the rump area of chickens raised for freshwater dry-fly feathers. Some novices make the mistake of trying to use these hackles for creating the bulkier bodies on baitfish patterns and tarpon flies when they should be using more rounded, fuller feathers. Save these long, narrow hackles to use as a side dressings on flies to add lateral lines and other markings.

Synthetic Materials

How do I begin—or end—talking about synthetic fly-tying materials? There's so many of these materials available that I can't possibly cover them all. Instead, let's look at broad categories; this will give you some idea about what you will find in the recipe sections of this book or at the local fly shop.

Synthetic hairs have taken the fly-tying world by storm. Poly Bear, Shimmer, Fluoro Fibre, and EP-Silky Fibers are just a few of the soft synthetic hairs

on the market. These materials are similar to craft fur but usually contain an added dash of flashy fibers. They are durable, easy to use, and the individual fibers have a natural taper like real fur. In the water, they breathe and give a fly a realistic swimming motion.

There is another class of synthetic hair material that is slightly stiffer. Ultra Hair and FisHair are the classics of this type of material. These long hairs are especially important for tying eel and epoxy patterns. It is difficult to substitute a soft hair for these harder hairs and vice versa. While I encourage you to experiment and try different materials, this is more difficult when substituting with these different types of synthetic hairs.

We can't discuss synthetic fly-tying ingredients without mentioning the wide array of new flash materials. Every fly shop and catalog carries Flashabou and Krystal Flash, and these materials have been widely copied by other manufacturers. In fact, aside from hooks and thread, I'll bet flash materials—Flashabou, Krystal Flash, and similar products—are found on more guides' patterns than any other material.

Quite a few of the patterns submitted by guides and other talented tiers incorporate synthetic tubing. This material was introduced as a substitute for Mylar tubing. Traditional Mylar tubing gives flies a flashy, scalelike appearance, but it isn't very durable. EZ Body, Corsair, Flexi-Cord, and Flexo tubing are made of woven monofilament and other tough fibers. These materials were originally manufactured as coverings for electrical wire and cables, but some inventive fly tier saw the possibilities; today almost all fly shops carry one or more brands of these new body materials.

chapter 2

Basic Flies

SOMETIMES SIMPLE IS BEST

It's natural to want to tie realistic imitations of the things fish eat. At fly-fishing shows, crowds of people gather around the tiers creating the most realistic patterns. It's fun to turn a bunch of fur, feathers, and other stuff into something that looks alive. In several of the following chapters, we'll examine a variety of very realistic looking patterns, but tying exact imitations of shrimp, crabs, and baitfish isn't how you learn the basics of fly tying. You must acquire the basic skills first, and then graduate to creating more complicated patterns.

This isn't to say that more natural-looking imitations catch more fish; in fact, for some inexplicable reason, simpler patterns sometimes out-fish realistic flies. But maybe the reason isn't so difficult to comprehend. The best explanation I've heard is that the more realistic you try to make a fly, the easier it is for a fish to see it as a forgery because the little things that are out of place send warnings to the predator. Make sense? I don't know: I'm not a fish.

What I do know is that oftentimes the simpler flies catch the most fish, or catch fish more regularly.

What do I mean by "simpler" flies? These patterns don't look like anything in nature, or they might resemble some natural type of food yet require only a couple of materials to construct (those are some of my favorite flies). Most of these flies rely on soft, realistic motion to convince fish that they're something good to eat.

From a tying standpoint, all of the flies in this chapter require only a few easily obtainable ingredients. You can create new patterns by substituting the colors of the materials and tie the flies in different sizes. Before you know it, you'll have a fly box full of great fish-catching patterns.

Let's tie a few of these basic flies. These patterns are winners because they catch fish and are relatively easy to tie. These flies teach the lessons for tying more complicated—and more realistic—patterns. This selection includes flies for fishing for tarpon, snook, and barracuda in the tropics as well as bluefish in the Northeast and striped bass on both coasts. It's a well-rounded selection that will quickly get you on the water and into fish.

Tying the Whistler

The Whistler, designed by Dan Blanton, is a great utility pattern that catches all kinds of predatory gamefish. I suppose it's most used for catching striped bass, but it does a number on bluefish, barracuda, and other species.

The key to the Whistler is the full hackle collar. This hackle "moves" water when the fly is fished with a stripping retrieve and sets off vibrations that help the fish locate the fly. The Whistler is a particularly effective pattern for fishing the turbid water along sand beaches and river estuaries; the fish can feel the fly moving through the water and they attack.

The Whistler is an excellent basic pattern for novice tiers because it's slightly larger and requires only a few common materials. You can also change the colors of the materials to create new patterns. The accompanying recipe specifies materials for tying a fairly standard Whistler, but mix and match

the colors as you see fit. If you subscribe to the old saw that says "bright day, bright fly–dark day, dark fly," then tie both dark- and light-colored Whistlers. When tied well, the Whistler is a lovely fly–even though it doesn't look like anything in nature.

The Whistler

Hook: Regular saltwater hook (such as the Varivas 990), sizes 2 to 3/0.

Thread: Black 3/0.

Tail: Black bucktail with strands of blue holographic Flashabou, flanked on each side with a grizzly saddle hackle.

Body: Red Crystal Chenille.

Collar: Grizzly saddle hackle.

Eyes: Large silver bead-chain.

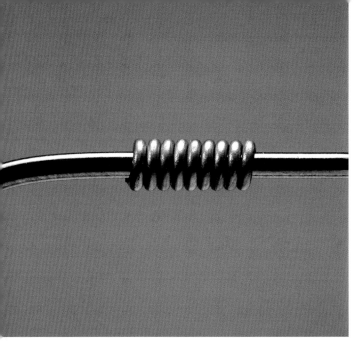

Step 1

The Whistler is a popular subsurface pattern, and you can add a few wraps of lead wire to the hook shank to help the fly sink deep. Several wraps of medium lead wire suffice.

Step 2

Start the thread near the end of the hook shank. Tie on a large bunch of black bucktail.

Step 3

Add several strands of fish-enticing flash material to the tail. Blue holographic Flashabou blends nicely with the black bucktail and brightens the tail.

Step 4

Grizzly saddle hackles give the Whistler a realistic barred appearance. Strip the fluffy fibers from the bases of two feathers. Tie a hackle to each side of the tail with the feathers curving in and the tips even.

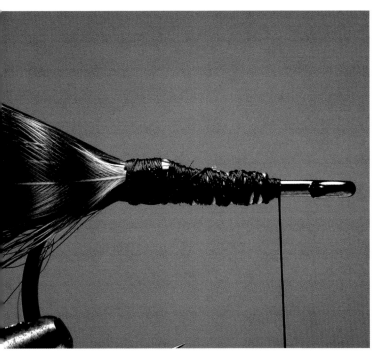

Step 5

Wrap the thread up and down the hook, covering the base of the tail and the wraps of lead wire. These thread wraps don't have to be real neat; they'll eventually be covered with other materials. Use firm wraps to create a strong underbody.

Step 6

Place a set of large bead-chain eyes on top of the hook shank in front of the wraps of lead wire. Secure the eyes to the shank with firm figure-eight wraps of thread. If you want to tie a really fast-sinking Whistler for fishing deep or in heavy current, you can substitute with lead dumbbell eyes.

Step 7

Tie on the end of a piece of red Crystal Chenille or Estaz at the base of the tail.

Step 8

Wrap the thread half way up the hook. Wrap the Crystal Chenille up the shank, tie off, and clip the excess. Use closely spaced wraps of Crystal Chenille to fully cover the thread underbody.

Step 9

Select another grizzly saddle hackle. Strip the fluffy fibers from the base of the feather. Tie the hackle to the hook in front of the Crystal Chenille.

Step 10

Wrap the hackle up the hook shank. Make closely spaced wraps to completely cover the thread under-body. Tie off the hackle directly behind the eyes.

Step 11

Pass the thread in front of the bead-chain eyes. Make a neat thread head and clip. Coat the thread head with cement. The Whistler is a large pattern that appeals to striped bass and other meat-eating fish. The bead-chain eyes add weight to the front of the fly and the Whistler bobs up and down when stripped through the water. The large, full hackle moves a lot of water, helping fish to locate the fly.

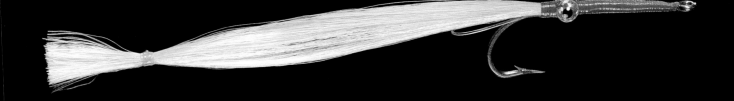

Tying the 'Cuda Fly

Needle fish are a common baitfish in the Florida Keys and other tropical waters. They are a favorite food among tarpon and barracuda. While I said many of the patterns in this chapter do not look like anything a fish might eat, the thin, long profile of the 'Cuda Fly is very similar to a needlefish. I also said that all of the flies in this section are easy to tie and require only a few materials; this is definitely true of the 'Cuda Fly.

The body of the 'Cuda Fly and many similar patterns are typically tied using some bright–you might say "gaudy"– colored material. For this example I'm using bright green and yellow FisHair to form the long body extending beyond the hook; the head of the fly is orange thread. These colors are typical of the 'Cuda Fly. Go figure.

'Cuda Fly

Hook: Long-shank saltwater hook (such as the Mustad 34011), size 2.

Thread: Orange flat-waxed nylon.

Body: Yellow and bright green FisHair (you may substitute with another brand of similar synthetic hair).

Eyes: Small or medium yellow dome eyes.

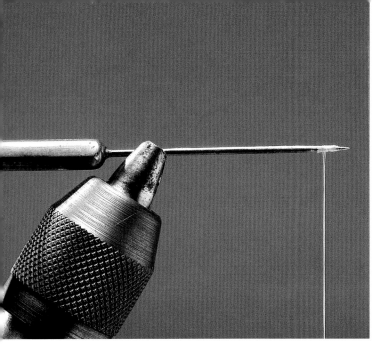

Step 1

Start the 'Cuda Fly by making the tail. Place a sharp object such as a needle or bodkin in your vise. Start the thread on the tapered end of the needle.

Step 2

Tie a bunch of yellow FisHair on the end of the needle.

Step 3

Select another color of FisHair; in this example I'm using bright green. Tie a bunch of this material on top of the first bunch. This will create a nice two-tone fly.

Step 4

Tie off the thread and clip. Coat the thread wraps with fresh cement; the cement should penetrate the thread and bind together the strands of FisHair. Allow the cement to dry for a few moments, and remove the tail from the needle.

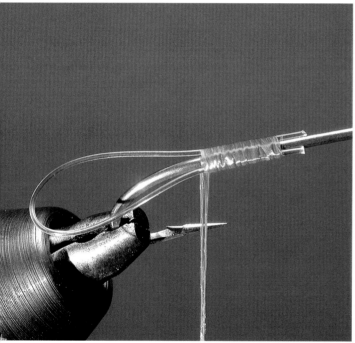

Step 5

The long, supple tail of the 'Cuda Fly might tangle around the hook when casting the fly. A small guard of 25- to 35-pound-test clear monofilament will help keep the tail from fouling around the hook.

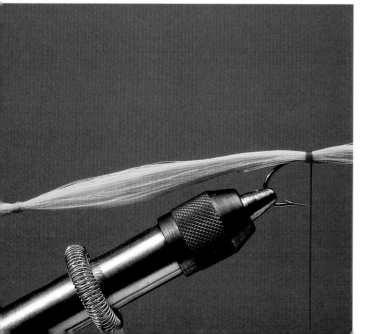

Step 6

Tie the tail on top of the hook shank. The tail should extend several inches beyond the end of the shank; the base of the tail should extend almost to the hook eye.

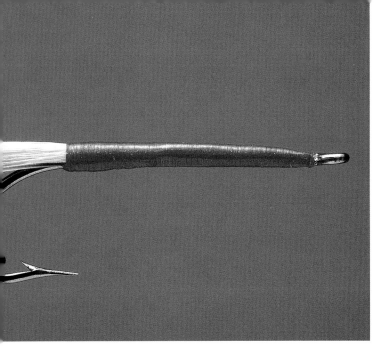

Step 7

Wrap the thread up the hook, binding the end of the tail to the top and sides of the shank. Use closely spaced wraps of thread and completely cover the FisHair. Flat-waxed nylon thread will create a smooth body. As you wrap the thread, however, it will twist tight and make a body with small ridges. To keep the thread lying flat, spin the spool counterclockwise after every dozen or so wraps; this will remove the twist. Tie off the thread and clip. Seal the body with two coats of head cement.

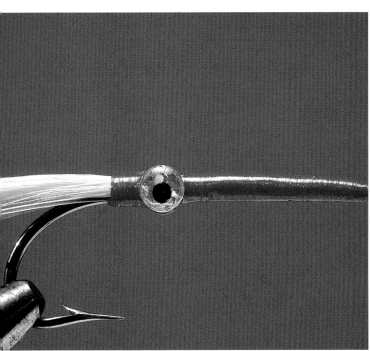

Step 8

Glue a medium-size dome eye to each side of the body. A drop of epoxy will secure the eyes to the fly.

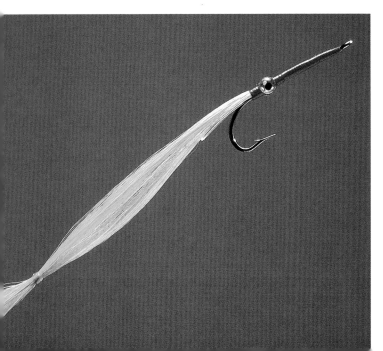

Step 9

The completed 'Cuda Fly has a very distinctive profile. It is a good choice where needlefish are an important baitfish.

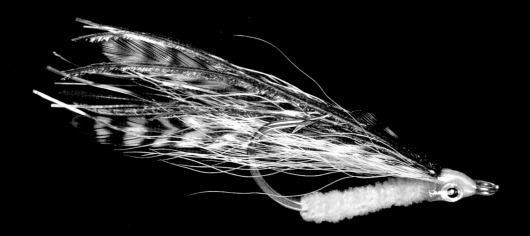

A Basic Flats Fly

Chico Fernandez, one of our sport's most famous anglers, uses the Bend-Back series of flies to catch redfish, bonefish, and a variety of other species in the Florida Keys and similar waters. This is another type of fly that can be tied in different sizes and colors. Be sure to tie a few Bend-Backs if you plan to wade the flats. This is a particularly good design for fishing where aquatic grass is a problem; the Bend-Back fishes hook-point-up and catches fewer weeds.

Bend-Back

Hook: Regular saltwater hook (such as the Mustad 34007), sizes 1 to 3/0. Bend up the first one-quarter inch of the hook shank. You can also purchase hooks especially designed for tying Bend-Backs and similar flies (such as the Tiemco TMC411S).

Thread: Yellow 3/0.

Body: Yellow chenille.

Wing: Yellow and chartreuse bucktail, strands of silver Flashabou, and peacock herl. A grizzly saddle hackle is tied on each side of the wing.

Eyes: Small silver adhesive eyes.

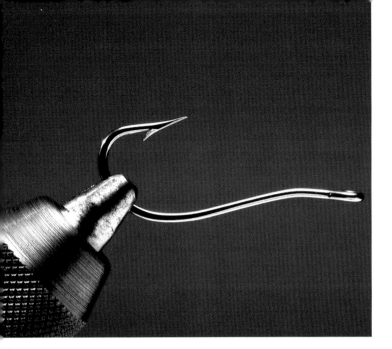

Step 1

The first step to tying the Bend-Back occurs before you go to the vise. Slightly bend the hook shank up: work carefully, use a needle-nose pliers, and place the bend about one-quarter inch from the hook eye. This slight bend causes the hook to flip over and ride with the point facing up. If you prefer, you can also purchase hooks designed for tying Bend-Backs.

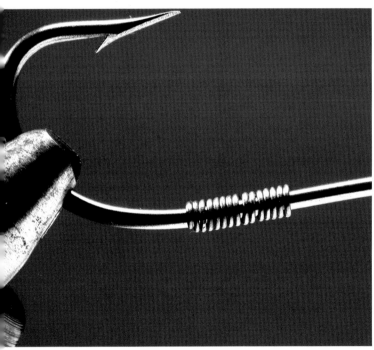

Step 2

If you want the fly to sink a little more quickly, add about ten wraps of medium lead wire in the middle of the hook shank.

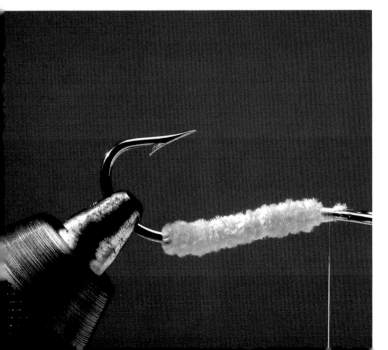

Step 3

Tie a piece of yellow chenille at the end of the hook shank. Wrap the thread up the shank to the beginning of the bend. Don't wrap beyond the bend; leave the front of the shank bare for tying on the wing. Wrap the chenille up the shank to form the body of the fly. Tie off and clip the excess chenille.

Step 4
Tie a small bunch of yellow bucktail to the top of the fly. This forms the first layer of the wing.

Step 5
Tie a small bunch of chartreuse bucktail on top of the wing.

Step 6
Select two grizzly saddle hackles. Hold the hackles on the sides of the bucktail wing. The hackles should be slightly longer than the bucktail. Clip the hackles to length and strip a few fibers from the base of each feather. Tie a hackle onto each side of the wing.

Step 7
Tie several strands of silver Flashabou on top of the wing.

Step 8
Tie a bunch of peacock herl to the top of the wing.

Step 9
Wrap a neat thread head. Tie off and clip the thread. Coat the head with a drop of cement. Allow the cement to dry before finishing the head; this might be a good time to start another fly.

Step 10

Place an adhesive eye on each side of the thread head. If gamefish really do key in on the eyes of their prey, they'll love the eyes on this Bend-Back.

Step 11

Coat the head and eyes with five-minute epoxy. The epoxy gives depth to the eyes and makes a very durable head.

Step 12

The completed Bend-Back is a simple fly that really catches fish. Because it fishes hook-point-up, it's a good pattern to use around mangroves and other places that snag flies. Change the colors of the materials to tie a whole collection of Bend-Backs.

Chartreuse & White Seducer
tied by Capt. Chris Dean
Miami, Florida

The Seaducer is a favorite pattern among many salt-water fly anglers. Capt. Chris Dean, who fishes Biscayne Bay and Flamingo, says "this is my favorite snook and baby tarpon fly. When tied with a wire weed guard, it's also a great flats redfish pattern."

Hook: Mustad 34007, size 1/0.
Thread: Chartreuse flat-waxed nylon.
Wing: Three white neck hackles on each side of the fly and strands of silver Flashabou.
Hackle: Palmer wrap a combination of white neck and saddle hackle up the hook shank.
Collar: Chartreuse saddle hackle.
Weed guard: No. 5 stainless-steel leader wire.

Red & White Bend-Back
tied by Capt. Chris Dean
Miami, Florida

"This is a variation of a red-and-white bucktail used for redfish back in the '60s," says Capt. Dean. "The original fly had no body and was tied on a standard hook. I changed the pattern to a Bend-Back and added the monofilament body. I use this fly for redfish in very shallow water. The bend-back style and very heavy wing make it weedless."

Hook: Tiemco TMC411S, size 1/0.
Thread: Red flat-waxed nylon.
Underbody: Silver Mylar tinsel.
Body: 40-pound-test clear monofilament.
Wing: White bucktail with strands of silver Flashabou.
Collar: Two red saddle hackles.

Deceiver
tied by Capt. Jim Ellis
West Barnstable, Massachusetts

Capt. Ellis shows that you can teach an old dog new tricks—or change and improve a time-honored fly pattern. Ellis's Deceiver is based on Lefty's Deceiver. Capt. Ellis substituted Poly Bear for the usual bucktail wing and belly, and he glues on large holographic dome eyes. Cape Cod's big striped bass and bluefish had better watch out!

Hook: Mustad 37160S, size 5/0.
Thread: Clear monofilament thread.
Tail: Six white saddle hackles. Tie on the tail and add a drop of Softex to the base of the feathers (this will stiffen the tail). Add a few strands of pearl Flashabou.
Belly: Pearl-white Poly Bear.
Sides: Smoky-olive Poly Bear.
Back: Peacock Angel Hair.
Throat: Fluorescent orange Fluoro Fibre.
Eyes: Large holographic dome eyes.

Ice Cream Cone
tied by Justin Krul
New Fairfield, Connecticut

Justin Krul isn't a fishing guide; he's a fine young man who has a fly-tying show on his local public-access television network, and that's pretty cool. Justin's dad, Jim, is the proprietor of English Angling Trappings, one of the most complete catalogs of unusual and hard-to-find fly-tying items. The Ice Cream Cone is a good striped bass fly, but it also does a number on hickory shad.

Hook: Regular saltwater hook, size 2.
Thread: White 3/0.
Head: Large silver cone.
Tail: Arctic fox tail hair.
Body: The butt ends of the tail fibers.
Rib: Silver wire.
Wing: Arctic fox tail hair.
Collar: Ice Chenille.

See-Through Deceiver
tied by Capt. Gary Graham
Los Barriles, Mexico

Capt. Graham designed the See-Through Deceiver to catch roosterfish, jack crevalle, dorado, tuna, and skipjack, just a few of the many species swimming the waters of Baja, Mexico.

Hook: Gamakatsu 18411 bait hook.
Thread: Monofilament or white flat-waxed nylon.
Tail: Pearl Flashabou.
Body: White bucktail with a natural grizzly saddle hackle on each side.
Wing: Strands of pearl saltwater Flashabou and olive bucktail.
Head: Coat the base of the white and olive bucktail with Softex.
Eyes: Red dome eyes.

Llamaceiver
tied by Bob Lindquist
East Patchogue, New York

Bob is an expert saltwater fly fisher and one of the most popular tiers on the winter fly-fishing show circuit. His Llamaceiver is another variation on the ever-popular Lefty's Deceiver. According to Bob, you can tie the Llamaceiver in a variety of sizes and colors to "catch anything that swims, fresh or salt."

Hook: Gamakatsu SL11-3H, sizes 6 to 2/0.
Thread: Monocord or flat-waxed nylon (use the Monocord for tying larger flies).
Belly & Wing: The entire body is made of llama hair mixed with strands of flash material such as Glimmer. Your choice of colors to match the local baitfish.
Throat: Red llama hair or some synthetic hair.
Eyes: Painted on the sides of the thread head.

Stringbean
tied by Capt. Roy String
Sarasota, Florida

Interested in catching snook at night? Capt. String can show you the way. He uses his Stringbean to catch snook in the evening, and for sight-casting to snook and redfish. While he uses arctic fox fur to tie his fly, you may substitute with lamb's wool.

Hook: Regular stainless-steel hook, size 4.
Thread: Chartreuse 3/0.
Tail: Arctic fox tail hair and strands of rainbow Krystal Flash.
Body: Ice Chenille.
Wing: Arctic fox tail hair.

The Nothin' Honey
tied by Capt. Ron Kowalyk
Ft. Myers, Florida

The Nothin' Honey is a good utility fly for fishing in Florida. Capt. Kowalyk uses this pattern to catch redfish, snook, spotted sea trout, and baby river tarpon.

Hook: Mustad 3407, sizes 2 and 1/0.
Thread: White flat-waxed nylon.
Tail: Strands of pearl Krystal Flash, white bucktail, and chartreuse bucktail (Capt. Kowalyk sometimes substitutes red, gray, brown, and pink for the chartreuse).

C.H. Woolly Bugger Express
tied by Capt. Larry Kennedy
St. Simons Island, Georgia

Capt. Larry Kennedy has been fishing and exploring Georgia's coastline since childhood. He uses his C.H. Woolly Bugger Express to catch the area's jacks, ladyfish, sharks, "and just about everything in our coastal waters."

Hook: Mustad 34011, size 2.
Thread: Red 3/0.
Head: Large gold cone.
Tail: Black marabou.
Body: Black Krystal Chenille.
Hackle: Black saddle hackle palmer-wrapped over the body.

'Cuda Killer
tied by Capt. Lenny Moffo
Big Pine Key, Florida

The 'Cuda Killer is a simple pattern you'll want to have the next time you fish the mangroves and other barracuda haunts. The extra-small bead-chain eyes allow the fly to ride hook-point-down.

Hook: Regular saltwater hook, size 2/0.
Thread: Chartreuse Monocord.
Tail: Chartreuse bucktail with strands of pearl Flashabou, three chartreuse saddle hackles on each side of the bucktail, and one narrow grizzly hackle on each side of the tail.
Collar: Chartreuse marabou.
Head: Bright red chenille.
Eyes: Extra-small silver bead-chain.

Frank's Roosterfish Fly
tied by Capt. Frank Oblak
Miami, Florida

Frank Oblak specializes in walk-in fishing for peacock bass, snook, tarpon, and redfish. He has used this pattern for catching roosterfish from the beach.

Hook: Regular saltwater hook, size 2.
Thread: White 3/0.
Tail: White and blue Aunt Lydia Rug Yarn, tied to the hook and combed out. Add a few strands of your favorite silver flash material.
Collar: A blue marabou tip on each side of the hook.
Head: Pearl Krystal Chenille.
Eyes: Extra-small dumbbell eyes.
Weed guard: 30-pound-test monofilament.

TYING BAITFISH PATTERNS

Big fish eat little fish: that's a proposition on which I think we can all agree. Small baitfish make up the bulk of the diets of most large predator gamefish—the same big fish we hope will eat our flies. As a result, you'll probably tie more imitations of baitfish than any other patterns. But there are exceptions to this rule.

If you specialize in casting to bonefish or permit, you might lean toward dressing crabs and other patterns that imitate the bait most commonly found on the sand and marl flats. And if you have the coin to hire a big boat and go offshore for marlin and sailfish, you'll want to fill a box with giant flies that might measure 12 inches or longer ("big fish eat little fish" is relative, and a 200-pound marlin likes a pretty

big fly). For the rest of the sportfish we pursue— bluefish, striped bass, barracuda, tarpon, yellowtail, false albacore, snook, and others too numerous to list—the most common patterns imitate smaller baitfish.

What are we trying to imitate with our baitfish patterns? Silversides, anchovies, menhaden, alewives, herring, tinker mackerel, smelt, ballyhoo, needlefish, and spearing are all common baitfish pursued by gamefish, and there are patterns that imitate all of these species. The guides and tiers I contacted in researching this book sent great patterns that imitate all of these baitfish. Later in this chapter you'll find the flies created by those expert guides and tiers; all of these patterns are worth carrying in your fly box.

Tying the Bay Anchovy

Many knowledgeable Northeast guides place the bay anchovy near the top of their lists of important baitfish: striped bass, false albacore, bonito, and other species feed on this common bait. The beauty of learning to tie the Bay Anchovy is that this pattern can serve as a foundation for other similar small flies: just change the colors of materials to create patterns to match the small bait swimming in your local waters.

The Bay Anchovy pattern we are going to tie, which is closely based on the RM Bay Anchovy fly tied by Massachusetts guide Richard Murphy, has a head coated with epoxy. The amount of glue used on this pattern is very small; you'll have no trouble learning how to craft the head on this fly. The epoxy makes this fly very durable, an important characteristic shared by all of Murphy's patterns.

Be sure to tie a few Bay Anchovies for your next Northeast saltwater fishing trip. You'll have fast action using these little flies.

Bay Anchovy

Hook: Short-shank stainless-steel hook (such as the Varivas 990S), size 2.

Thread: Clear monofilament.

Underbody: Lead wire and pearl Mylar tinsel.

Belly: Two strands of red Krystal Flash.

Body: Olive arctic fox, pink arctic fox, and white arctic fox. Feel free to substitute with other soft natural or synthetic furs. The key word is "soft"; the material should have a flowing action in the water. Add a few strands of pearl Krystal Flash to make the body sparkle.

Eyes: Medium silver holographic adhesive eyes.

Gills: Red permanent marker.

Head: Five-minute epoxy.

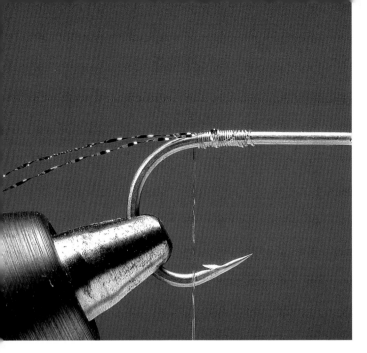

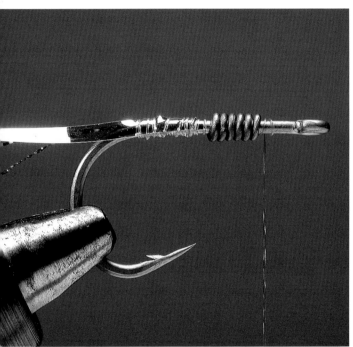

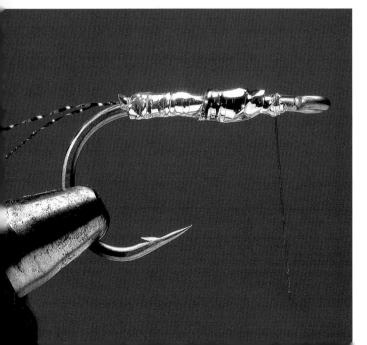

Step 1

Start the thread near the end of the hook shank. Tie two pieces of red Krystal Flash on top of the shank.

Step 2

Tie on a piece of pearl Mylar tinsel. Add six to eight wraps of medium lead wire to the hook shank.

Step 3

Wrap the pearl tinsel up the hook shank and over the lead wire. Tie off and clip the excess tinsel. This bit of tinsel will give the finished fly depth and flash.

Don't worry if the tinsel underbelly doesn't look neat (it's tough to wrap tinsel over lead wire); it will eventually get covered with epoxy.

Step 4

Tie a 2- to 3-inch-long bunch of arctic fox to the top of the hook shank. Arctic fox has a lot of short underfur; this is what helps keep the animal warm in its frigid environment. While it's common to pick out and discard the underfur when tying flies, don't remove the underfur this time; it will give the body a little bulk.

Step 5

A few strands of pearl Krystal Flash, tied on top of the arctic fox, give the finished body a dash of flash.

Step 6

Tie a few strands of pink arctic fox on top of the fly. Note that I cleaned the underfur from the long strands of pink hair; there should just be a slight pink tint running the entire length of the body.

Step 7

Tie a small bunch of olive arctic fox to the top of the fly. Do not remove the underfur from this bunch of material.

Step 8

Secure all of the fur with several firm wraps of thread. Tie off the thread and clip. Add a drop of cement to the thread to hold everything in place while you continue working.

Step 9

Mix a small batch of five-minute epoxy. Coat the head—about half way down the hook shank—with epoxy. Allow the epoxy to cure—not just harden—before proceeding. I usually tie a batch of Bay Anchovies, apply epoxy to the entire lot, and allow the glue to cure for twenty-four hours. If you work too fast and apply the second coat of epoxy before the first has a chance to cure, the finished head will appear dull and murky.

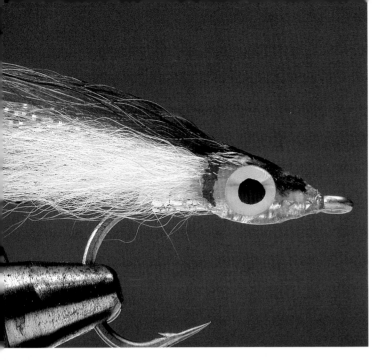

Step 10

Place a small adhesive eye on each side of the head. The gills are made with a red fine-tip permanent marker.

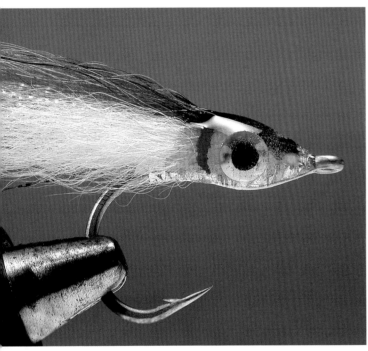

Step 11

Apply a second coat of five-minute epoxy to the head. This coat seals the eyes and gills, and gives the fly a nice finished look.

Step 12

The completed Bay Anchovy has all of the characteristics of a good small baitfish pattern: it's easy to tie, is durable, and has a fishy swimming motion in the water.

Tying Enrico's Peanut Bunker

The next pattern was not invented by a guide. Enrico Puglisi, of New York, sells a nice line of fly-tying materials ideal for creating saltwater patterns. I've watched Enrico tie flies at many shows, and I am impressed by the realism and obvious durability of his patterns. His Peanut Bunker is a good example.

A menhaden—commonly called a bunker or pogie—has a tall, narrow profile that is tough to imitate. Many salt- and freshwater baitfish have this profile. There are several ways to create this shape on a fish hook—Enrico's Peanut Bunker is just one solution.

I am tying the Peanut Bunker using EP-Ultimate Fibers, one of the materials in Enrico's family of products, but there are several other materials that will also work: Shimmer, Poly Bear, and Slinky Fibre are just a few of the substitutes you'll find in the local fly shop. If you want to keep things really simple, you can also substitute with long craft fur (note, however, that many synthetic fly-tying furs contain a dash of sparkle fibers that really add to the appearance of the finished fly).

EP-Ultimate Fibers do not contain any shiny fibers, so Enrico adds a dash of EP-Sparkle when he ties the body of the Peanut Bunker (I'll demonstrate this in the tying steps). Lite Bright is a good substitute for this material. You can also use this technique if you tie the Peanut Bunker with craft fur.

The gills on the Peanut Bunker are made out of red EP-Silky Fibers. Red SLF Hanks or a few strands of red Krystal Flash, even red yarn, are excellent substitutes.

There's one neat advantage about using EP-Ultimate Fibers and similar synthetic fibers: most of these materials can be easily colored with permanent markers. This means you can tie the entire body of a fly with one—maybe two—colors of hair, and then color the back or belly with permanent markers in the colors of your choice. Olive and light olive are popular for the backs of flies; pink and orange are often used for the bellies. You can also use a marker to add vertical bars and other realistic markings to your flies. Synthetic fibers have opened up a whole world of possibilities for creating realistic, durable, fish-catching flies.

Peanut Bunker

Hook: A regular stainless-steel saltwater hook (such as the Mustad 34007), sizes 2 to 3/0.

Thread: Clear monofilament.

Body: Polar white and gray EP-Ultimate Fibers, and silver EP-Sparkle (or your choice of synthetic hair and flash materials).

Gills: Red EP-Silky Fibers.

Eyes: Large silver holographic dome eyes.

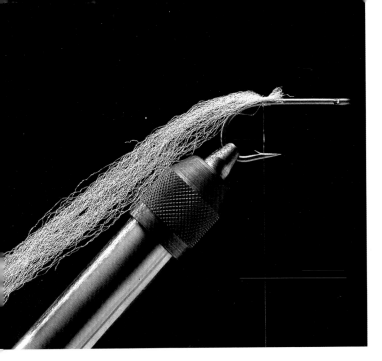

Step 1

Start the monofilament thread near the end of the hook shank. Tie a long, narrow section of white synthetic hair to the top of the shank. Since I learned about this pattern from Enrico Puglisi, I am using his EP-Ultimate Fibers; that's the least I can do.

Step 2

Tie a short section of red synthetic fibers to the bottom of the shank. The red fibers suggest the gills of the small bunker. It might seem early to tie on the gills, but the head of the fly fills the hook shank; if you tie on the gills later, they'll be too far forward.

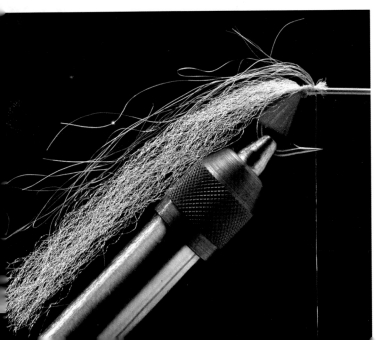

Step 3

Some synthetic hair materials have a dash of sparkle, but I need to add flash to the EP-Ultimate Fibers. Tie on several strands of silver flash material. I'm using EP-Sparkle, but Lite Bright is a good substitute.

Step 4

Tie a section of white synthetic hair on top of the flash material. Note that this strip of hair is slightly shorter than the first piece.

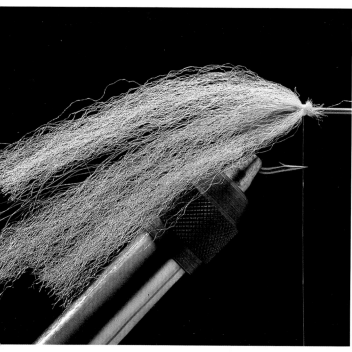

Step 5

Tie a section of white synthetic fibers to the bottom of the hook shank in front of the gills. Notice that I'm working up the hook shank. I'm also applying the materials to the top and bottom of the shank, not the sides. The profile of the bunker is long, tall, and narrow. You can simulate this appearance by tying the ingredients to the top and bottom of the hook.

Step 6

Tie another bunch of flash material to the top of the fly.

Step 7

Tie a section of gray synthetic hair to the top of the fly, and a section of white to the bottom. Add a few more strands of flash material to the top.

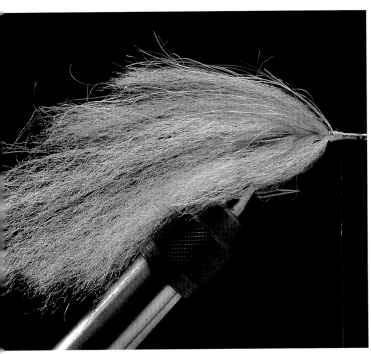

Step 8

Continue working up the hook, adding sections of gray hair to the top and white hair to the bottom of the shank. Add strands of flash material if necessary.

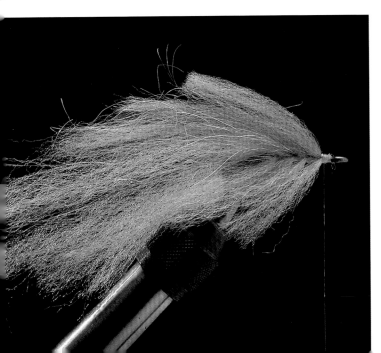

Step 9

In this photograph you can see that the sections of hair get shorter as I work up the hook shank. The red gills are just peeking through the body. The rough profile is long and tall, but the body has remained rather thin, just like a real bunker.

Step 10

Because I've tied the bunches of materials on only the top and bottom of the hook shank, we can see the wraps of thread. I honestly don't think the fish will mind, but I do. There's an easy way to tidy up the head of our fake fish. We'll do that in the next step.

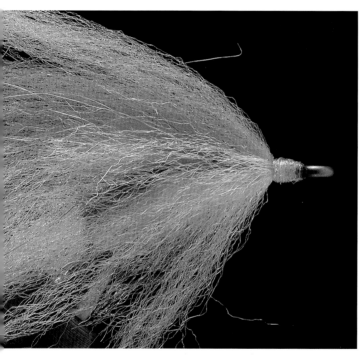

Step 11

Tie a short section of white synthetic hair—about equal to the length of the hook—to each side of the fly. These pieces of material hide those ugly thread wraps. Tie off the thread and clip. Coat the thread head with cement.

Step 12

Comb out the hairs. The rough, untrimmed fly has the profile of an outstretched hand.

Step 13

Clip the hairs to create the silhouette of the small bunker. It's easier to trim the hair by clipping forward from the tail of the fly.

Step 14

Glue a large silver holographic eye to each side of the head. If gamefish really do key in on the eyes of their prey, these holographic eyes will grab their attention.

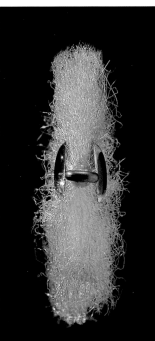

Step 15

The completed Peanut Bunker has the profile of the natural baitfish. The soft synthetic hair gives the fly a lot of fluid motion in the water.

Step 16

The front view of the Peanut Bunker. The fly is tall and narrow, just like a real bunker.

Lil' Hadden
tied by Capt. Gary Dubiel
Oriental, North Carolina

Capt. Gary Dubiel, who operates a guide service appropriately called Spec Fever, tied the Lil' Hadden to catch sea trout, redfish, flounder, striped bass, weakfish and Spanish mackerel. It's a good utility pattern.

Hook: Short-shank saltwater hook, size 6.
Thread: Clear monofilament.
Weight: Five to six wraps of medium lead wire covered with silver braid.
Body: White craft fur, pink craft fur, silver Krienik Flash-n-Tube, and green craft fur.
Head: Five-minute epoxy and medium holographic dome eyes.

Gotcha' Clouser
tied by Capt. James Ellis
West Barnstable, Massachusetts

Capt. Ellis believes in the effectiveness of circle hooks. His sparse Gotcha' Clouser is tied on an Eagle Claw circle hook.

Hook: Eagle Claw NT 2052 circle hook, size 1/0.
Thread: Clear monofilament.
Body: Bill's Bodi Braid wrapped on hook shank.
Wing: Tan and white bucktail with strands of pink Flashabou.
Eyes: Brass dumbbell eyes.

Baby Bunker
tied by Capt. James Ellis
West Barnstable, Massachusetts

Hook: Gamakatsu 208412, size 2/0.
Thread: Clear monofilament.
Body: Pearl blue Angel Hair forms the bottom
two-thirds of the fly, and rainbow Angel Hair is
tied on top.
Throat: Fluorescent orange Fluoro Fibre.
Eyes: Large silver holographic dome eyes glued to
the sides of the fly.

Silverside
tied by Capt. James Ellis
West Barnstable, Massachusetts

Hook: Eagle Claw NT2052 circle hook, size 1.
Thread: Clear monofilament.
Tail: Pearl Angel Hair with a bit of smoky olive Poly
Bear. Place a drop of Softex on the base of the tail
near the hook shank to stiffen the material.
Body: Silver Bill's Bodi Braid wrapped on the
hook shank.
Belly: Pearl Angel Hair.
Back: Smoky olive Poly Bear.
Throat: Fluorescent orange Fluoro Fibre.

Angel Hair Zonker
tied by Capt. James Ellis
West Barnstable, North Carolina

Hook: Eagle Claw NT2052 circle hook, size 1/0.
Thread: Clear monofilament.
Body: Pearl Bill's Bodi Braid.
Wing: Pearl Angel Hair.
Eyes: Small silver adhesive eyes, coated with a dab
of five-minute epoxy.

Baja Deepdiver
tied by Capt. Gary Graham
Escondido, California

Hook: Eagle Claw 413 jig hook, sizes 1/0 to 4/0.
Thread: Clear monofilament.
Weight: Twenty-five wraps of light lead wire.
Body: One white saddle hackle on each side of the
hook. White Super Hair or bucktail on the bottom of
the hook. Chartreuse Super Hair or bucktail on top
of the fly. Add strands of pearl saltwater Flashabou
to the top.
Eyes: Large silver, chartreuse, or red adhesive eyes.
Coat the head with five-minute epoxy.

Silverside Muddler
tied by Bob Lindquist
East Patchogue, New York

Tier Bob Lindquist says his Silverside Muddler "is my favorite fly for taking stripers sucking down silversides on a hot summer evening."

Hook: Gamakatsu SC15, size 1/0.
Thread: Flat-waxed nylon (body), Uni-Cord 7/0 (head). Since you don't see the thread on this pattern, color choice is optional.
Tail: Silver Glimmer sandwiched between white EP-Ultimate Fibers mixed with pearl blue Angel Hair and lime EP-Ultimate Fibers mixed with pearl green Angel Hair.
Head: Pale olive deer hair over white deer hair. The red gill line on the bottom of the fly is made with a red permanent marker.
Eyes: Small holographic adhesive eyes glued in place.

Bass Magic
tied by Capt. Bob Robl
Dix Hills, New York

Hook: Mustad 34001, size 1/0.
Thread: Black Monocord.
Tail: Red craft fur, two red hackles, and strands of red Krystal Flash.
Body: Medium red chenille.
Eyes: Large gold bead-chain.

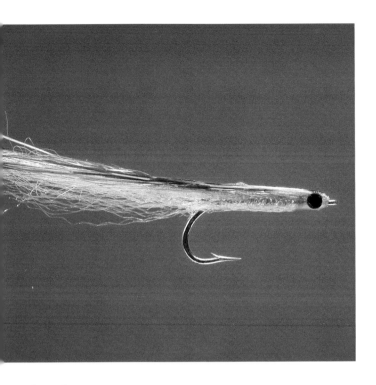

Spearing
tied by Capt. Ken Kuhner
Cold Spring Harbor, New York

Capt. Ken Kuhner ties his Spearing pattern to catch striped bass and bluefish.

Hook: Gamakatsu SL11-3H, size 2.
Thread: Clear monofilament.
Body: Pearl Bill's Bodi Braid.
Tail: White Slinky Fiber and strands of olive Flashabou.
Eyes: Small silver adhesive eyes.
Head: Apply a coat of five-minute epoxy over the entire body. The tail fibers are tied on behind the hook eye and pulled back as you apply the epoxy.

Bay Anchovy
tied by Capt. Ken Kuhner
Cold Spring Harbor, New York

The Bay Anchovy is a good fly to use during the autumn runs of bonito and false albacore.

Hook: Gamakatsu SL11-3H, size 2.
Thread: Tan, size 6/0.
Weight: Lead tape folded over the hook and cut to form the shape of the body.
Body: Pearl Bill's Bodi Braid.
Tail: Tan Polar Fiber and strands of gold Flashabou.
Eyes: Small silver adhesive eyes.
Head: Apply a coat of five-minute epoxy over the entire body. The tail fibers are tied on behind the hook eye and pulled back as you apply the epoxy.

RM Spitfire
tied by Rich Murphy
Georgetown, Massachusetts

According to Richard Murphy, the RM Spitfire is a very reliable and popular imitation of a variety of small forage fish common to Northeast inshore beaches and estuaries.

Hook: Tiemco TMC600 SP, size 1/0.
Thread: Clear monofilament.
Weight: 3/16-inch-diameter tungsten silver cone.
Tail: White Finnish raccoon, long natural polar bear, and strands of ultraviolet Krystal Flash.
Belly: Several strands of red Krystal Flash.
Wing: Pale olive bucktail, pale lavender bucktail, pink bucktail, and pale olive saddle hackles. Tie strands of herring back ultraviolet Krystal Flash on top of the wing, and pearl ultra-violet Krystal Flash on each side of the fly.
Head: Coat the cone head and the base of the wing and belly with epoxy. Color the top of the head with a bronze permanent marker, and the top one-quarter of the head with a dark olive marker. Place a silver adhesive eye on each side of the head. Apply another coat of epoxy.

RM Bay Anchovy
tied by Richard Murphy
Georgetown, Massachusetts

The RM Bay Anchovy is a good imitation of a real bay anchovy. The Finnish raccoon, which comprises the bulk of the body, is soft and has a lot of action in the water.

Hook: Trey Combs Big Game Hook, size 2.
Thread: Clear monofilament.
Weight: Lead tape covered with silver Mylar tape.
Tail: Rainbow Krystal Flash over white Finnish raccoon.
Belly: Four strands of red Krystal Flash.
Wing: Pale olive bucktail over very sparse pink Polar Fibre. Tie two strands of rainbow Krystal Flash on the top and sides.
Eyes: Small silver adhesive eyes.
Head: Coat the head with five-minute epoxy. Allow the epoxy to cure. Color the top of the head with an olive permanent marker and add the eyes. Apply a second coat of five-minute epoxy.

Boomer
tied by Richard Murphy
Georgetown, Massachusetts

The Boomer is designed to imitate a variety of common juvenile baitfish including alewives and herring.

Hook: Tiemco TMC600 SP, size 1/0.
Thread: Clear monofilament.
Weight: 3/16-inch tungsten silver cone.
Belly: Strands of red Krystal Flash.
Tail: White Finnish raccoon, natural polar bear hair, strands of pearl ultraviolet Krystal Flash, and then another bunch of white Finnish raccoon.
Wing: Peacock herl, dark olive bucktail, pale lavender bucktail, and pale pink bucktail. Strands of herring back ultraviolet Krystal Flash on top, and strands of pearl ultraviolet Krystal Flash on each side.
Eyes: Large silver adhesive eyes.
Head: Coat the head with five-minute epoxy. Allow the epoxy to cure. Color the top of the head with a bronze permanent marker, and color the top one-quarter with a dark olive permanent marker. Add the eyes. Apply a second coat of epoxy.

RM Flatside 2
tied by Richard Murphy
Georgetown, Massachusetts

The RM Flatside 2 catches a wide variety of game: striped bass, bluefish, bonito and false albacore in the Northeast; redfish and jacks in the Southeast; and roosterfish and small tuna along the Pacific coast.

Hook: Tiemco TMC911S, size 2/0.
Thread: Clear monofilament.
Weight: Lead tape covered with silver Mylar tape and clipped to shape.
Body: Large pearl EZ Body tubing. Thread the hook into the tubing. Tie the tubing off behind the hook eye. Flatten the tubing and color with permanent markers: bronze on the top half, lavender on the top one-third, dark olive on the top one-quarter, and pink on the belly. Add a black false eye spot on each side of the body.
Tail: Light gray marabou and rainbow Krystal Flash inserted into the end of the tubing. Insert the tail materials and start the thread on the end of the tubing. Tighten the thread to close the tubing. Tie off and clip the thread.
Head: Coat the eyes and head with five-minute epoxy.

Green Ghost
tied by Capt. Jim White
Coventry, Rhode Island

The Green Ghost is a great pattern for catching fluke, sea bass, and striped bass.

Hook: Long-shank saltwater hook, size 3/0.
Thread: Black, size A.
Underbody: Worm rattle.
Tail: White bucktail, white Comes Alive, pearl blue Polar Flash, and gold Polar Flash.
Body: Black Opal Tubing (the material actually looks green).
Throat: Red Flashabou.
Eyes: Medium silver holographic adhesive eyes.
Head: Coat the large thread head and eyes with five-minute epoxy.

Five-Feather Herring
tied by Capt. Doug Jowett
Brunswick, Maine

Capt. Jowett specializes in fishing the waters of Maine and Cape Cod. The Five-Feather Herring is a good pattern for fishing these areas when the striped bass and bluefish are turned on to real herring.

Hook: Long-shank saltwater hook, size 3/0.
Thread: Clear monofilament.
Underbody: Worm rattle.
Tail: White saddle hackles splayed in opposite directions.
Wing: Chartreuse FisHair, pearl saltwater Flashabou, and peacock herl.
Eyes: Medium gold adhesive eyes.
Gills: A band of orange tying thread.
Head: Five-minute epoxy.

DJ Hi-Ti
tied by Capt. Doug Jowett
Brunswick, Maine

The Hi-Ti method of tying is simple: tie on a small amount of body material, make several wraps of thread, and tie on another bunch of materials. Continue adding bunches of material up the hook shank. The last step is to trim the body to shape. The completed fly has a tall, narrow profile. The DJ HI-Ti is a good example of this type of pattern.

Hook: Regular saltwater hook, size 1/0.
Thread: White, size A.
Tail: White FisHair.
Body: White FisHair tied on top of the hook shank using the Hi-Ti method. Tie on the FisHair and then clip the body to shape. Tie strands of silver holographic Flashabou on the sides of the body.
Eyes: Medium gold adhesive eyes glued to the sides of the head.

Kris's Bonito Special
tied by Capt. Kris Jop
Marion, Massachusetts

Kris's Bonito Special is a general baitfish imitation that catches bonito and false albacore. This fly will work wherever saltwater gamefish key in on small baitfish.

Hook: Regular saltwater hook, size 4.
Thread: Clear monofilament.
Wing: White Polafibre, chartreuse Polafibre, yellow Polafibre, and strands of silver Flashabou.
Head: Witchcraft silver gill plates.
Eyes: Small yellow dome eyes. Place an eye on each gill plate and coat with five-minute epoxy.

chapter 3 guide flies

Feather Pup
tied by Capt. Lenny Moffo
Big Pine Key, Florida

Designed for catching tarpon and cobia, the Feather Pup is another baitfish pattern that will appeal to gamefish everywhere.

Hook: Regular saltwater hook, size 3/0.
Thread: Brown Monocord.
Tail: Brown bucktail with strands of gold Flashabou. Tie two brown grizzly hackles and one golden brown grizzly hackle on each side of the tail. Tie the hackles curving out.
Collar: Brown marabou.
Head: Brown wool.
Eyes: Yellow plastic doll eyes.

Sea Pup
tied by Capt. Lenny Moffo
Big Pine Key, Florida

This cousin to Capt. Moffo's Feather Pup features a durable strip of rabbit fur for the tail. This is another pattern that will catch fish just about anywhere.

Hook: Regular saltwater hook, size 3/0.
Thread: Tan Monocord.
Tail: A tan rabbit strip and strands of pearl Krystal Flash.
Collar: A tan rabbit strip wrapped around the hook shank. Tie a pheasant body feather on each side of the fly and curving out.
Head: Tan wool.
Eyes: Orange doll's eyes.

Utility Minnow
tied by Capt. Lenny Moffo
Big Pine Key, Florida

Capt. Moffo uses the Utility Minnow to catch a wide variety of fish, including baby tarpon, sea trout, snook, barracuda, jacks, and bluefish.

Hook: Regular saltwater hook, size 2/0.
Thread: White Monocord to tie the belly and wing of the fly; complete the fly using orange Monocord.
Belly: White bucktail.
Wing: Strands of gold Flashabou, chartreuse bucktail, a golden brown grizzly hackle on each side of the wing, and strands of peacock herl.
Head: Orange Monocord.
Eyes: Yellow adhesive eyes.

Jail Bait
tied by Capt. Lenny Moffo
Big Pine Key, Florida

The Jail Bait imitates a pinfish, a common baitfish in the Florida Keys.

Hook: Regular saltwater hook, size 2/0.
Thread: White Monocord to tie the wing of the fly, and black Monocord to finish the fly.
Wing: White bucktail, strands of pearl Krystal Flash, olive bucktail, light brown bucktail, strands of olive Krystal Flash, and strands of peacock herl. Lateral markings are black permanent marker.
Head: Black Monocord coated with epoxy.
Eyes: Medium gold adhesive eyes.

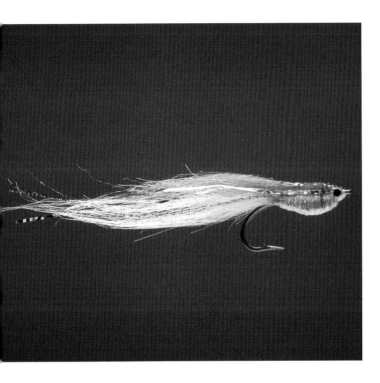

Big-Bellied Silverside
tied by Capt. John Haag
Brookhaven, New York

"The Atlantic silverside is a very prominent bait in the Northeast and loved by all predatory fish," says Capt. Haag. *"They range from two to five inches in length, and I tie this pattern as long as my materials allow. I fish it with a sinking line, and I explore different depths by counting longer with each cast before I begin retrieving the fly."* Tie all of the materials to the hook and then coat the body and base of the wing with epoxy.

Hook: Mustad 34007, size 2/0.
Thread: White flat-waxed nylon.
Tail: Light gray Fly Fur.
Body: 3/32-inch-thick foam tied to the bottom of the hook shank. Wrap pearl Bodi Braid over the foam.
Wing: Light gray Fly Fur topped with olive Fly Fur.
Lateral lines: Silver holographic Flashabou and black Krystal Flash.
Eyes: Extra-small silver adhesive eyes.

Glimmer Bunker
tied by Capt. John Haag
Brookhaven, New York

Hook: Eagle Claw 254SS, sizes 2/0 to 4/0.
Thread: White flat-waxed nylon.
Tail: Silver Glimmer.
Body: Pearl Glimmer, live-glow Comes Alive, light blue Bozo Hair and sea blue Bozo Hair. To help the fly maintain its shape, lightly coat the base of the wing and throat with Softex or Soft Body.
Throat: Polar-bear Bozo Hair.
Eyes: Medium silver dome eyes.

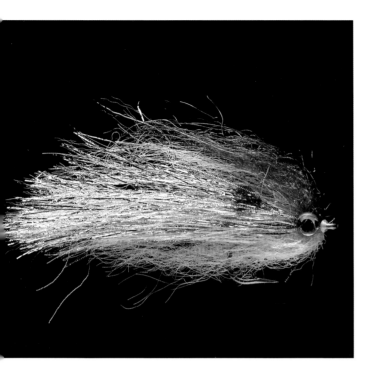

Glimmer Pinfish
tied by Capt. John Haag
Brookhaven, New York

Hook: Eagle Claw 254SS, size 2/0.
Thread: White flat-waxed nylon.
Tail: Silver Glimmer.
Wing: Live-glow Comes Alive, and silver and olive Bozo Hair. To help the fly maintain its shape, lightly coat the base of the wing and throat with Softex or Soft Body.
Throat: Silver Bozo Hair.
Eyes: Medium gold dome eyes.

Glimmer Herring
tied by Capt. John Haag
Brookhaven, New York

Capt. Haag says that the Glimmer Herring is a "great fly when the alewives are spawning in the spring and the herring are migrating in the fall."

Hook: Eagle Claw 254SS, size 3/0.
Thread: White flat-waxed nylon.
Tail: Silver holographic Flashabou.
Wing: Silver Glimmer, pearl Glimmer, olive Comes Alive, silver Bozo Hair and olive Bozo Hair. To help the fly maintain its shape, lightly coat the base of the wing and throat with Softex or Soft Body.
Throat: Silver Bozo Hair.
Eyes: Medium gold dome eyes.

No-Bay-Vy
tied by Capt. John Haag
Brookhaven, New York

"This pattern is tied to represent a bay anchovy. I fish it most often using an intermediate-sinking line. The No-Bay-Vy is a very effective albacore pattern. When the albacore have pushed anchovies to the surface and are in a feeding frenzy, I toss this right in the middle and strip as fast as I can."

Hook: Eagle Claw 254SS, size 2.
Thread: Tan 6/0.
Wing: Rainbow Glimmer; chartreuse bucktail; pink, lavender, and olive marabou; and strands of peacock herl.
Throat: Tan arctic fox tail.
Head: Pearl Mylar tinsel coated with epoxy.
Eyes: Painted chartreuse with black pupils.

Rainfish
tied by Capt. John Haag
Brookhaven, New York

Rainfish, which are actually bay anchovies, are a favorite food of false albacore and bonito. The Rainfish is a good pattern to use when these special gamefish are turned on to real anchovies.

Hook: Eagle Claw 254SS, sizes 6 to 2.
Thread: Tan 6/0.
Tail: Tan Fly Fur.
Body: Silver Mylar tinsel.
Wing: Tan, pink, chartreuse, and royal blue Fly Fur, and rainbow Glimmer.
Cheeks: Pearl Mylar tinsel, one piece on each side of the wing and trimmed at an angle toward the hook point. After the eyes are attached, coat the entire head with epoxy.
Eyes: Extra small yellow adhesive eyes.

Spring Lance
tied by Capt. John Haag
Brookhaven, New York

*Capt. Haag uses this pattern in the upper part of the
water column tethered to the end of an intermediate-
sinking line. When chased by predators, real sand lance
burrow into the soft bottom; Capt. Haag then fishes this
pattern with a deep-sinking line. Fish the Sand Lance
with a slow, deliberate retrieve.*

Hook: Eagle Claw 066SS, sizes 6 and 4.
Thread: White flat-waxed nylon.
Tail: White arctic fox and Gray Ghost Krystal Flash.
Body: Gray Ghost Krystal Flash wrapped on the
hook shank.
Wing: Polar bear and Kelly green Ultra Hair; pearl,
peacock, and black Krystal Flash.
Eyes: Small silver adhesive eyes. After the eyes are
attached, coat the entire body and the base of the
wing with epoxy.

Woolly Mullet
tied by Capt. John Haag
Brookhaven, New York

*According to Capt. Haag, "Mullet are a favorite food of
striped bass. This pattern often catches the bigger bass
close to the bottom. Fish this pattern using a sinking-tip
line and with the idea of putting the fly at the same
level as the fish you're after."*

Hook: Eagle Claw 054SS, size 2/0.
Thread: White flat-waxed nylon.
Tail: White arctic fox, white and olive bucktail, pearl
and silver Glimmer, light blue and gray Ultra Hair,
and strands of peacock herl.
Head: White sheep's wool colored on top with
brown, green, and olive permanent markers; use a
red permanent marker to make a mouth under the
hook eye and color the belly.
Eyes: Medium silver dome eyes glued to the sides of
the head.

Woolly Mummichog
tied by Capt. John Haag
Brookhaven, New York

Hook: Eagle Claw 054SS, sizes 1 and 1/0.
Thread: Yellow flat-waxed nylon.
Tail: Yellow and olive bucktail; tan, light blue, and
fuchsia Ultra Hair; yellow Glimmer; and strands
of peacock herl.
Head: Yellow sheep's wool colored on top with green
and brown permanent markers; use a red permanent
marker to color the belly.

JP's Mini Mack
tied by Jeffrey Pierce
Scottsville, New York

*Some anglers say that too much flash can scare away
fish, but not Jeff Pierce. He says that "the flash in the
Mini Mack brings fish up from the deep in a hurry."*

Hook: Mustad C71SS, size 4/0.
Thread: White 3/0.
Body: Underside of the hook: silver and pearl
Flashabou Mirage. On top of the hook: silver and
blue Flashabou Mirage. Apply a small amount of
Softex or a similar product to help the fly maintain
a tall, narrow profile. Color the top of the thread
head with a blue permanent marker, and color the
bottom of the thread head with a red permanent
marker.
Gills: Red Flashabou Mirage.
Eyes: Large silver dome eyes.

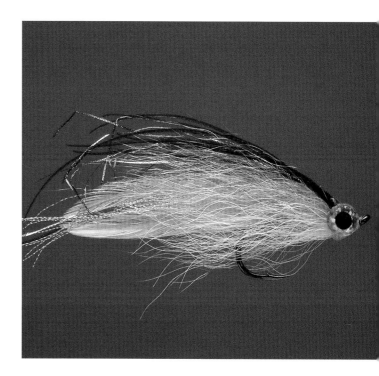

JP's Flying Fish
tied by Jeffrey Pierce
Scottsville, New York

This is another of Jeff's very inventive patterns. He's used the Flying Fish to catch dolphin, yellowfin tuna, skipjack tuna, blackfin tuna, false albacore, king mackerel, amberjack, barracuda and red snapper. It's a good utility pattern wherever gamefish feed on real flying fish.

Hook: Mustad C70S D, size 6/0.
Thread: White 3/0.
Body: Large pearl Flexi-Cord. Silver and blue Flashabou Mirage is inserted in the top of the body. The top of the body is colored with a green permanent marker. The tail is clipped to shape, epoxied, and colored with permanent markers. Color the gills and under the head with a red permanent marker.
Fins: White hackles.
Eyes: Large silver dome eyes.

Tuna Snack
tied by Carter Andrews
Crooked Island, Bahamas

Hook: Mustad 92554 NPBLN, size 5/0.
Thread: White 3/0.
Tails: Four white hackles and strands of pearl Krystal Flash.
Body: Pearl Mylar braid.
Belly: White bucktail.
Wing: Tan Poly Bear, white bucktail, olive Glimmer, and peacock herl.
Eyes: Extra large silver holographic dome eyes.

chapter 4 — Tarpon Flies

TARPON FLIES: IN A CLASS OF THEIR OWN

I must confess that I originally grouped the following discussion of tarpon flies in the chapter on tying baitfish patterns. Most tarpon flies have the general profiles of baitfish and are stripped through the water like baitfish flies, and it seemed natural that they be lumped in with the other baitfish patterns. Besides, no chapter was being dedicated to flies designed to catch a single species of gamefish, and I didn't want to start making exceptions. My editor, however, had different ideas.

I'm fortunate to have an editor that has some considerable experience fishing salt water. He argued that tarpon flies and fishing techniques are unique, and god knows these fish are in a class of their own. He convinced me that tarpon flies really do constitute a separate family of flies deserving consideration on their own merits.

There's no denying the fact, however, that many guides and tiers get their inspiration for tying tarpon flies from needlefish, a favorite forage of tarpon. The long, sleek needlefish form, epitomized by Stu Apte's famous Stu Apte Tarpon Fly, has been used to create hundreds of similar patterns. Let's look at this family of flies by tying two of Apte's patterns. I have also included the recipes for a large number of additional tarpon flies, most submitted by guides from Florida. If you live in tarpon country or plan to visit, you'll want to have a selection of these patterns.

Tying the Stu Apte Tarpon Fly

As a family, tarpon flies have a look all their own. They are sleek and sparse, and have some form of collar to move water. "Move water" is one of the favorite phrases of Chico Fernandez, a noted saltwater fishing authority living in Miami. Chico has caught more tarpon than I'll probably see in my lifetime. I've been privileged to have had several discussions with him about fly design, and he insists that a good tarpon pattern moves water and sets off vibrations when it is stripped. These vibrations help the tarpon locate the fly. This same concept—moving water—applies to many other types of flies, especially those that are used along beaches, jetties, and other places where there is crashing surf. But even when fishing in the quiet back bays and among the mangroves, a fly that moves water will give you an edge in catching a tarpon.

If imitation is the sincerest form of flattery, then some fly patterns have a lot of admirers. Lefty's Deceiver and the Clouser Minnow have been used by countless tiers as the basis for creating new patterns. The Stu Apte Tarpon Fly, developed by the noted Florida angler and guide whose name adorns the pattern, has also spawned numerous imitations. Let's tie a classic Stu Apte Tarpon Fly,

and then we'll look at a variation. The Stu Apte Tarpon Fly was featured on a United States postage stamp several years ago.

Note that the saddle hackles used to tie the tail of the Stu Apte Tarpon Fly have full, rounded tips. Many saddle hackles are long and skinny; these feathers come from chickens grown for dry-fly hackle. While those pencil-thin feathers are used on many flies, including some tarpon patterns, they are out of place on the Stu Apte Tarpon Fly. You might find the correct hackles on skins sold as streamer capes, but packaged strung hackle is probably your best source.

Stu Apte Tarpon Fly

Hook: Long-shank stainless-steel hook (such as the Mustad 34011), sizes 2 to 4/0.

Thread: Bright orange flat-waxed nylon.

Wing: Two bright orange and four bright yellow saddle hackles.

Collar: One bright orange and one bright yellow saddle hackle.

Body: Bright orange flat-waxed nylon tying thread.

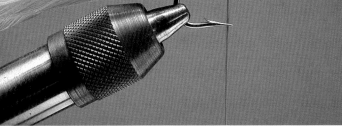

Step 1

Select two bright orange and four bright yellow saddle hackles. These feathers should have a full, rounded appearance—they should not be long and skinny. Strip the fluffy fibers from the base of each feather. Place the orange hackles together curving out. Place two yellow hackles on each side of the orange hackles.

Start the thread about two-thirds of the way down the hook shank. Place the bunch of hackles on top of the end of the hook. Pinch the hackle stems to the hook shank, and make three or four light wraps of thread to hold the feathers in position. Adjust the hackles until you are pleased with the appearance of the tail (note that the tail is about twice the length of the hook shank). Now make several firm wraps of thread to lock the feathers into position.

Step 2

We're looking down at the tail of the Stu Apte Tarpon Fly. Note how the feathers in the tail flair out. This gives the fly a nice breathing action when it is stripped through the water.

Step 3

Select one bright orange and one bright yellow saddle hackle. Strip the fluffy fibers from the base of each feather. Tie the hackles to the hook at the base of the tail. Wrap the feathers together up the shank. Make a full collar that will "push water" and create vibrations when the fly is fished. Tie off and clip the excess hackle tips.

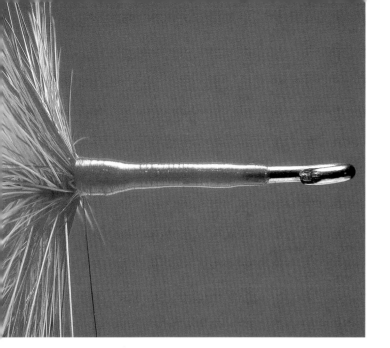

Step 4

Cover the stubs of the hackle tips with neat wraps of thread. Wrap the thread up the shank to create the famous snout of the Stu Apte Tarpon Fly. The thread will twist tight while you wrap, so occasionally spin the bobbin counterclockwise to unwrap the thread; this will allow the thread to lie flat and create a smooth body. Whip-finish and clip the thread.

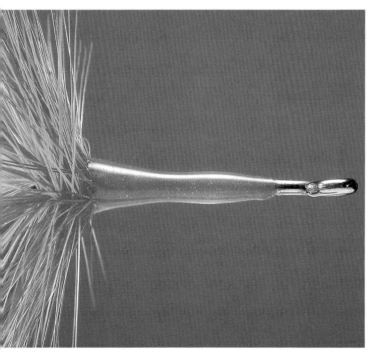

Step 5

Coat the thread body with a thin layer of five-minute epoxy. I know most tiers don't go to this trouble, but the epoxy makes the fly more durable and gives it a polished appearance. You may simply seal the thread body with head cement.

Step 6

The completed Stu Apte Tarpon Fly. Remember seeing this pattern on the postage stamp? It's one of our sport's most famous flies, and should be in your fishing kit the next time you go tarpon fishing.

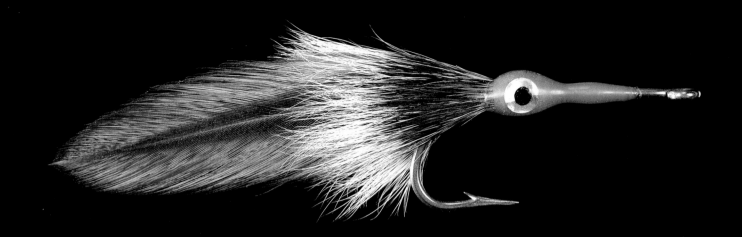

Tying Apte II

Apte II is a variation of the original Stu Apte Tarpon Fly. It's sort of a racy looking little creation, and it is widely used by knowledgeable tarpon guides and anglers. Apte II is the basis for many other flies; substitute the colors of materials to create new patterns. Call your guide well in advance of your fishing trip and ask which colors he prefers; most experienced guides have strong preferences for flies of certain colors and sizes. Prepare an assortment of patterns using the guide's recommendations.

Stu Apte painted the eyes on the Apte II, but I am using small sheet adhesive eyes coated with epoxy. Both methods work, but I like the glow of the shiny eyes and the durability of epoxy.

Apte II

Hook: Long-shank saltwater hook (such as the Mustad 34011), sizes 2 to 4/0.

Thread: Bright orange flat-waxed nylon.

Wing: Two furnace or brown saddle hackles. Note that these feathers have broad, rounded tips.

Collar: Gray squirrel tail hair.

Body: Bright orange flat-waxed nylon tying thread.

Eyes: Small gold adhesive eyes.

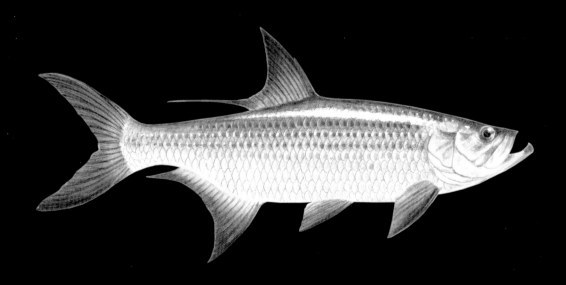

Step 1

Select two furnace saddle hackles (you may substitute with brown feathers); choose feathers that have broad, rounded tips. Strip the fluffy fibers from the base of each feather. Place the hackles back-to-back (curving in) with the tips even. Hold the hackles over the hook. Continue stripping fibers from the feathers until the length of the completed tail is about one and one-half to two times the length of the hook shank.

Start the thread near the end of the hook shank. Tie the hackle tail to the end of the shank: make two loose wraps of thread, adjust the feathers so the tail lies flat with the hook bend, and secure the tail with three or four firm wraps of thread.

Step 2

Clip a fairly large bunch of hair from a gray squirrel tail. Clean any underfur or short fibers from the base of the bunch. Place the bunch of fur on top of the hook shank; the tips of the hair extend almost one-half the length of the hackles. Hold the hair in place with two loose wraps of thread.

Step 3

Tighten and make two additional firm wraps of thread. Tightening the thread rolls the hairs to the far side of the hook; this is good. As the hairs roll to the other side, they will cover most of the base of the tail. This technique is similar to spinning deer hair, but squirrel hair does not flair. In the photo we're looking at the far side of the fly; note how the hair is covering the top, base, and bottom of the tail.

Step 4

As I tightened the thread, the hairs rolled around the hook, leaving this small gap at the base of the tail.

The next step is to fill this gap with a small bunch of hair.

Step 5

Clip a small bunch of squirrel tail hair. Clean out any underfur and short fibers from the base of the bunch. Tie the hair in the gap in the collar. Secure this bunch with a couple of very firm wraps of thread.

Step 6

Clip the butt ends of the squirrel tail hair at an angle. This will help the thread make a smooth transfer from the base of the hair collar to the hook shank.

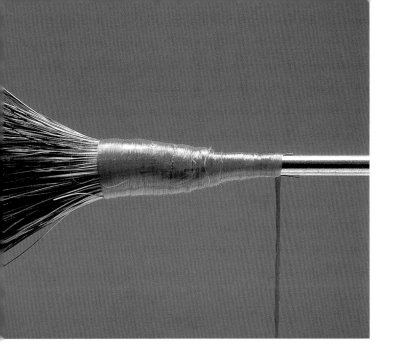

Step 7

Wrap the thread from the base of the collar to the hook shank. Use firm tension on the thread to lock the collar in place.

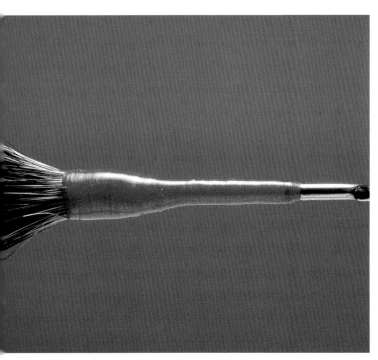

Step 8

Wrap the thread up the hook shank. Flat-waxed nylon thread creates a smooth body. As you work, however, the thread will twist and not lie flat. The solution? After every ten to twelve wraps, spin the bobbin counterclockwise to remove the twist. On the fly in the photo I wrapped the thread up the shank, wrapped the thread back to the base of the hair collar, and then wrapped back up the shank, creating a neat body containing three layers of thread. I then tied off and clipped the thread.

Coat the body with five-minute epoxy. Allow the epoxy to cure before proceeding (you might want to tie a batch of Apte II's and apply the epoxy on all of the flies in one sitting).

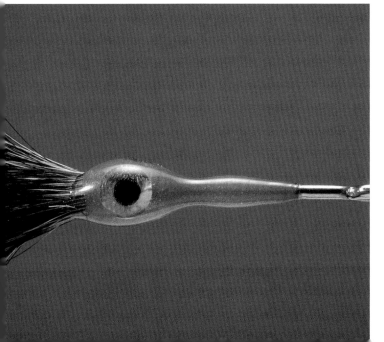

Step 9

Place an adhesive eye on each side of the head of the fly at the base of the collar. Apply a second coat of epoxy. Except for the feather tail and hair collar, this fly is damn near indestructible!

Step 10

The completed Apte II. The full hair collar will move a lot of water when the fly is stripped through the water, helping the tarpon to find your offering. This pattern is another in the series of Stu Apte's famous series of saltwater flies.

Green Hornet
tied by Capt. Dexter Simmons
Sugarloaf Shores, Florida

Hook: Regular saltwater hook, size 2.
Thread: Chartreuse, size 6/0.
Tail: Four grizzly hackles (divided into two bunches and splayed) and strands of pearl Flashabou.
Collar: Soft chartreuse fur such as a rabbit strip wrapped around the collar.
Eyes: Small gold adhesive eyes.
Head: Built-up with tying thread. Coat the head and eyes with five-minute epoxy.

Black Death
tied by Capt. Dexter Simmons
Sugarloaf Shores, Florida

Hook: Regular saltwater hook, size 2.
Thread: Black, size 6/0.
Tail: Two red and two black hackles (divided into two bunches and splayed with the red hackles on the inside of the tail), and strands of silver holographic Flashabou.
Collar: Soft gray fur such as a rabbit strip wrapped around the hook shank.
Eyes: Small red adhesive eyes.
Head: Built-up with tying thread. Coat the head and eyes with five-minute epoxy.

Bob's Bread and Butter
tied by Capt. Bob Rodgers
Tavernier, Florida

Bob's Bread and Butter is a simple yet beautifully tied tarpon fly. The soft materials—marabou and a rabbit strip—give the fly a lot of motion in the water. A loop of 25-pound-test Mason hard monofilament is tied to the end of the hook shank to prevent the rabbit-strip tail from fouling around the hook.

Hook: Regular saltwater hook, sizes 1/0 to 3/0.
Thread: Hot orange, size 6/0.
Tail: Tan rabbit Zonker strip and strands of pearl Flashabou.
Collar: Yellow marabou.

Bob's Tarpon Crab
tied by Capt. Bob Rodgers
Tavernier, Florida

This impressionistic crab pattern catches tarpon year-round.

Hook: Regular saltwater hook, sizes 1/0 to 3/0.
Thread: Hot orange, size 6/0.
Tail: Strands of orange Krystal Flash. Tan grizzly saddle hackle tips splaying in opposite directions (two or three hackle tips per side).
Eyes: 100-pound-test monofilament, melted and dipped in epoxy.
Collar: Tan and blue marabou.

Green Zima
tied by Tim Borski
Islamorada, Florida

Tim Borski uses the Green Zima to catch tarpon throughout the spring and summer. The craft-fur tail and wing make it a very durable pattern.

Hook: Regular saltwater hook, size 2/0.
Thread: Black flat-waxed nylon.
Tail: Chartreuse craft fur. The lateral markings are brown permanent marker.
Collar: Brown saddle hackle.
Wing: Chartreuse craft fur.

Red Death
tied by Capt. Len Roberts
Islamorada, Florida

The Red Death is designed for catching tarpon.

Hook: Mustad 7766, size 1.
Thread: Black, size 6/0.
Tail: Short strands of pearl Flashabou and six black saddle hackles (divided into two bunches and splayed). Tie a thin natural grizzly hackle on the outside of the black hackles.
Collar: Red hackle.
Eyes: White and black fabric paint.
Head: Built-up with black tying thread. Coat the head and eyes with five-minute epoxy.

Len's Tarpon Ocean Runner
tied by Capt. Len Roberts
Islamorada, Florida

Capt. Roberts is enjoying a growing reputation on the famous flats around Islamorada. His Tarpon Ocean Runner is an excellent pattern for catching the area's tarpon, and will probably work wherever tarpon swim.

Hook: Mustad 7766, size 3/0.
Thread: Black, size 6/0.
Tail: A short piece of SLF Hanks under six furnace saddle hackles (note that the hackles are divided but not splayed).
Collar: Cream marabou.
Eyes: White and black fabric paint.
Head: Built-up with tying thread. Coat the head and eyes with five-minute epoxy.

Malzone's Blondie
tied by Capt. Dan Malzone
Tampa, Florida

Capt. Malzone is a two-time IGFA world-record holder for tarpon, and Malzone's Blondie is typical of the patterns he uses to catch these large fish in the waters near Homosassa, Florida.

Hook: Owner Aki, size 4/0.
Thread: Fluorescent orange flat-waxed nylon.
Tail: Six cree saddle hackles (divided into two bunches and splayed).
Collar: Platinum blonde squirrel tail.
Head: Built-up with thread and coated with five-minute epoxy.

chapter 4 guide flies

Malzone's Black Death
tied by Capt. Dan Malzone
Tampa, Florida

Hook: Owner Aki, size 4/0.
Thread: Black flat-waxed nylon.
Tail: Six black saddle hackles (divided into two bunches and splayed).
Collar: Black squirrel tail.
Head: Built-up with tying thread and coated with epoxy.

Malzone's Purple Demon
tied by Capt. Dan Malzone
Tampa, Florida

Hook: Owner Aki, size 4/0.
Thread: Black flat-waxed nylon.
Tail: Six purple badger saddle hackles (divided into two bunches and splayed).
Collar: Black squirrel tail.
Head: Built-up with tying thread and coated with five-minute epoxy.

Tarpon Toy
tied by Capt. Lenny Moffo
Big Pine Key, Florida

*Capt. Moffo splits his time between Florida and Belize.
His extensive experience fishing for most of the major
species of saltwater gamefish—tarpon, bonefish, permit,
barracuda, and others—gives him special insight into
what makes a good saltwater fly. He has proven his flies
throughout the Florida Keys and Caribbean.*

Hook: Regular saltwater hook, size 3/0.
Thread: Tie the tail and body of the fly with brown
Monocord, and switch to orange Monocord to
complete the head of the fly.
Tail: Long red squirrel tail fibers with strands of gold
Flashabou, and two furnace hackles on each side.
Collar: A dark gray rabbit strip wrapped around the
hook shank.
Head: Orange Monocord coated with epoxy.
Eyes: Small yellow adhesive eyes.

Black Fly
tied by Capt. Lenny Moffo
Big Pine Key, Florida

*We've all seen flies turned into art, but here's a fly
that was inspired by a piece of art. Vaughn Cochran,
the manager of Turneffe Island Lodge in Belize, is one
of the finest sporting artists around. Vaughn created a
black-and-white illustration of a tarpon fly for a logo,
and Capt. Moffo used the illustration as inspiration
for this fly. It turned out the Black Death is a great
pattern for catching tarpon.*

Hook: Regular saltwater hook, size 3/0.
Thread: Black Monocord.
Tail: Black bucktail with three black hackles on
each side. Tie two narrow grizzly hackles on each
side.
Collar: Large black hackle.
Eyes: Black plastic beads.
Head: Black Monocord coated with epoxy.

chapter 5

Shrimp, Squid & Eels

OTHER FLIES THAT CATCH BIG FISH

I believe the old angler's adage: big fish eat little fish. At least I believe it most of the time.

While smaller fish make up the bulk of the diets of our favorite gamefish, many of the species we pursue also feed on a variety of other forage. Depending upon where and what you fish for, shrimp, squid, and eels occupy an important place on a saltwater gamefish's dinner table. Squid and eels are used in the Northeast to catch striped bass and bluefish. Shrimp catch their share of Northeast fish—patterns that

imitate grass shrimp are particularly effective when the stripers are working estuary shores—and they become increasingly important as you work your way down the coast. Indeed, shrimp flies are excellent for fishing inshore for redfish and other species from the Florida Keys west to Corpus Christi, Texas.

I enjoy tying flies that imitate shrimp, squid, and eels. They're something out of the ordinary; a trout angler would never carry one of these patterns in his fly box. And these flies are a lot of fun to tie.

Tying Art's Shrimp

Some time ago, Art Scheck, the editor of *Saltwater Fly Fishing* magazine, and I spent a weekend tying flies at the spectacular International Gamefish Association headquarters in Ft. Lauderdale, Florida (the IGFA center is a wonderful living shrine to all forms of fishing). I spent my time making small baitfish patterns; Art entertained the crowd by tying simple, realistic-looking shrimp imitations.

During a break in my tying, I spent half an hour watching Art make these neat little crustaceans. They defy the general rule about making fairly realistic-looking flies. A lifelike shrimp pattern is typically difficult and time-consuming to make, but Art's fly is marvelously simple; it doesn't take a lot of different materials or advanced tying skills, and it does a very nice job of imitating a real shrimp.

We wrapped up our tying kits on Sunday afternoon and left Ft. Lauderdale for Key West. After two days of showing folks how to tie flies and cast, we planned to reward ourselves with a bit of fishing. The next morning, before heading to the nearby flats, we stopped at a well-known tackle shop to get the latest fishing report. A bait fisherman was there buying live shrimp, and I watched the proprietor of the store dip a net into a large concrete tank and scoop out the shrimp. He withdrew the net and dropped the wiggling crustaceans into a clear plastic bag. I couldn't help but notice how much Art's tan shrimp matched the real thing.

Art's Shrimp requires only a few materials. The long antennae, one of the chief features of a shrimp, can be made out of plain rubber legs, but I prefer something with a little flecking such as Sili Legs.

The head and body of the fly are made of dubbing. Since the body dubbing will be picked out to thicken the fly and create the appearance of legs, select a shaggy, long-fiber material. In the tying photos I am using standard SLF dubbing.

The shell back of Art's Shrimp is made from a strip of clear plastic. Art Scheck, always the practical do-it-yourselfer, clips strips from a plastic sandwich bag, but Wapsi's Thin Skin (there are other similar products) is meant for the job.

Art's Shrimp

Hook: Long-shank saltwater hook (such as the Mustad 34011), sizes 8 to 1/0.

Thread: Size 3/0, color to match the body.

Antennae: Rubber hackle material, color to match the body.

Head: A tuft of dubbing.

Eyes: Burned monofilament.

Body: Dubbing (pink, tan, and orange are excellent colors).

Shell back: A strip of transparent plastic.

Rib: 10-pound-test clear monofilament (or Vinyl Rib in a color to match the body).

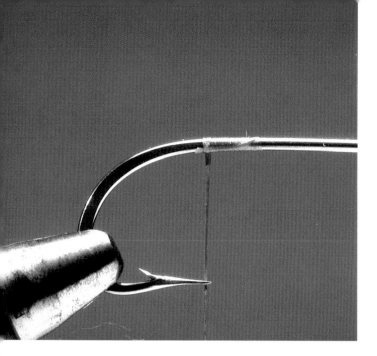

Step 1

Start the thread near the end of the hook shank. Lay down a small base of thread on which to tie the head of the shrimp. This layer of thread will help keep the dubbing, which forms the head of the shrimp, from spinning around the smooth hook shank.

Step 2

Tie a small pinch of dubbing at the end of the hook shank. Secure the dubbing with two or three firm wraps of thread.

Step 3

Fold back the dubbing so all of the fibers extend out over the bend of the hook. Secure the dubbing with two or three firm wraps of thread.

Step 4

Clip two 3-inch-long pieces of rubber hackle material. I am using a product called Sili Legs because I like the more natural flecking in the material. Tie an antennae on each side of the fly near the top of the hook.

Step 5

Now it's time to make the eyes. Select a size of monofilament that matches the size of shrimp you're tying. The most common mistake is using monofilament that is too small. I'm using a size 1 hook, so I've selected 60-pound-test mono. The spool costs about two bucks and contains enough material to make eyes for hundreds of flies. Twenty-five-pound-test monofilament is about the lightest I use for tying flies on size 8 hooks.

Step 6

Clip a 4-inch-long piece of monofilament. Use a butane lighter or a long wooden match to melt a ball of monofilament on each end of the line. Keep turning the line as you work to prevent the molten plastic from falling off the end. This is another reason I use heavy monofilament: I can create large eyes and still control the molten plastic.

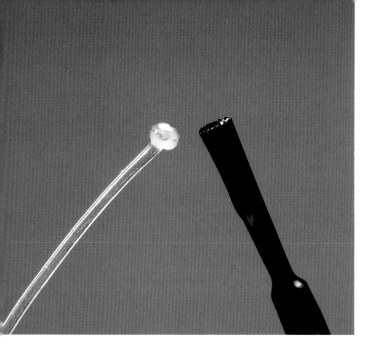

Step 7

Paint each eyeball with a drop of black fingernail polish. This will make the eyes stand out and call to the fish: "Come and get it!"

Step 8

A set of completed eyes for Art's Shrimp. These eyes are actually on each end of the same strand of monofilament. I started with a 4-inch-long piece of mono, and melted an eyeball onto each end of the line. I'll spend an evening just making sets of eyes for future tying sessions; it's something simple to do when I don't have time to tie complete flies. I store the sets of eyes in a plastic sandwich bag.

Step 9

Tie an eye onto each side of the fly. Note that the eyeballs extend beyond the end of the hook. This is important so that the eyes don't become covered by the body dubbing.

Step 10

Tie a piece of 10-pound-test monofilament or Vinyl Rib to the bottom of the fly. It's important to position the monofilament on the bottom of the hook so that it doesn't interfere with other parts of the fly when you later wrap the material up the shank to form the rib.

Step 11

Form a large dubbing loop of thread. Wrap the bobbin of tying thread up the hook shank (don't crowd the hook eye—study the photo).

If you've tied freshwater flies, this dubbing loop is a little longer than what you're probably used to using. The finished fly on this size 1 hook will have a long body—the dubbing will have to cover the entire hook shank from the base of the shrimp's head to the hanging thread—and my dubbing loop (which extends below the bottom of the photo) is about 5 inches long.

Rub dubbing wax on the loop. Insert dubbing into the loop.

Step 12

Twist the dubbing loop closed to form a chenille-like rope of dubbing.

Step 13

Wrap the dubbing up the hook shank to form the body of the fly. Tie off and clip the excess dubbed thread.

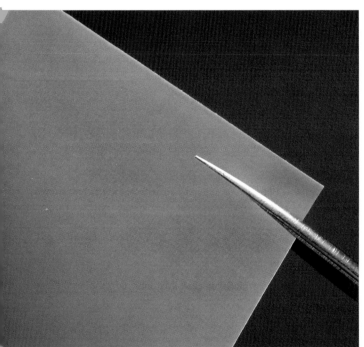

Step 14

Now you're ready to make the shell back of the shrimp. You can make the shell out of a clear sandwich bag, but I prefer using Thin Skin. Thin Skin is a flexible, translucent plastic that is more durable than the sandwich bag. Thin Skin comes on a heavy paper backing which you peel from the plastic. Start by cutting a ¼-inch-wide strip of Thin Skin. I select a color of Thin Skin that matches the color of the dubbed body.

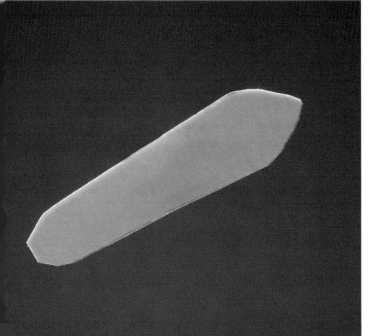

Step 15

Taper the ends of the Thin Skin. The broad end will form the shell over the head of the shrimp. The shaped shell back is about 1¼ inches long.

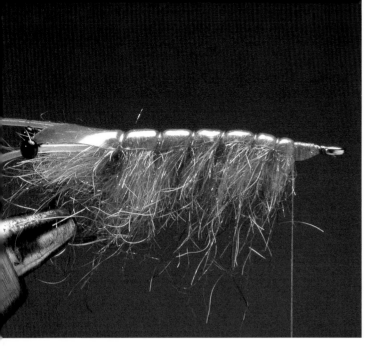

Step 16

Brush the dubbing on top of the fly down the sides of the shrimp. Place the shell back on top of the fly. Spiral-wrap the monofilament up the hook to form the rib of the fly, securing the shell back to the fly and creating a nice segmented appearance. Brush down any dubbing that gets bound on top of the shell by the rib. The shell will want to roll onto the far side of the fly as you wrap the rib, but just keep pulling the Thin Skin back on top as you wrap the monofilament. Tie off and clip the excess monofilament.

Now you can see why it was important to tie the beginning end of the monofilament to the bottom of the fly several steps ago: if it was tied on the top or side, it would interfere with the shell back when wrapping the rib. Remember: a good fly tier plans ahead.

Step 17

Whip-finish and clip the thread. Place a drop of cement on the thread head to secure everything in place.

Some of the body dubbing will get bound down when wrapping the rib. Use a bodkin to pick out this dubbing.

Step 18

The completed Art's Shrimp. The soft dubbing will pulsate with every twitch of line, giving the fly a nice swimming action. This durable, easy-to-tie pattern works wherever gamefish feed on shrimp.

Tying the RM Shortfin Squid

A couple of years ago, in a river estuary near my home in Maine, I'd been catching good numbers of striped bass using all of the usual flies: Lefty's Deceivers, Clouser Minnows, and similar patterns we've all used dozens of times. Playing those stripers was fun, but fishing for them was becoming a bit of a bore. I searched through my fly boxes and found a couple of squid patterns. I had used these flies farther down the coast, but not in Maine. It was time to give them a try.

I cast one of the squid flies into the middle of the falling tide and gave it a gentle twitch. After a few moments, the line slowly tightened. Fish on! I played and released the bass, and made another cast. I let the fly sink into the current and repeated the easy, pulsating retrieve. I quickly hooked another fish. Again and again, the slow retrieve of the bushy squid pattern tricked fish; it also rekindled my interest and I continued fishing.

Richard Murphy's RM Shortfin Squid is more complicated to tie than the pattern I used that autumn morning, but it's also a much nicer fly. Follow the tying steps and work slowly, and I know you'll end up with a fishable squid. Murphy is so meticulous in his tying methods that I feel I must discuss the differences between his version of the pattern and my own. Most of the changes I made are due to the selection of materials at my local fly shop. I went to the store to buy the materials to tie the fly as specified by Murphy, but they didn't have all of the ingredients and I made substitutions. The most important change is in the type of large-diameter tubing I am using for the fly body. Murphy uses a more loosely woven variety that can be easily stretched, expanded, and contracted. It is made of fine monofilament and is very durable. The type of tubing I found at the fly shop is equally durable, but is not quite as flexible. It also contains strands of narrow pearl Mylar tinsel. Another difference is the material I wrap on the hook for the underbody. Murphy uses plain pink chenille; I chose sparkly Crystal Chenille.

RM Shortfin Squid

Head

Thread: White 3/0.

Tentacles & head: Rainbow Krystal Flash, white or gray Sili Legs or a similar product, gray ostrich herl, gray marabou, and medium pearl EZ Body tubing. Color the EZ Body with blue and pink permanent markers.

Eyes: Large silver dome eyes.

Body

Hook: A 4X-long saltwater hook (such as the Tiemco TMC900S), size 4/0.

Thread: Fine monofilament.

Underbody: Pink chenille or Crystal Chenille.

Overbody: Flexo tubing.

Fins: Pearl Krystal Flash and gray marabou.

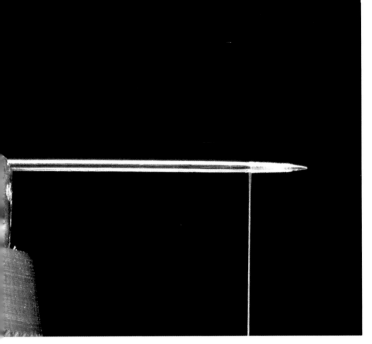

Step 1

I tie the RM Squid in two steps: the head and then the body. Begin the head by tying the materials to the tip of a dubbing needle. Place the needle securely in the vise. Wrap a base of thread on the tapered tip of the needle.

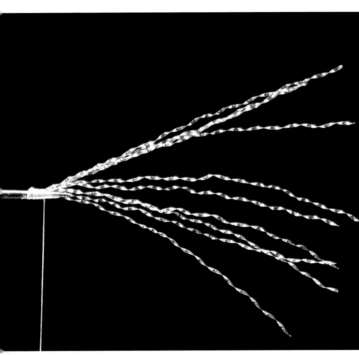

Step 2

Tie several strands of rainbow Krystal Flash to the needle. It's easier and less wasteful to fold three or four long strands of Krystal Flash over the thread, and then wrap the thread onto the hook. Clip the Krystal Flash to length later.

Step 3

Tie several long strands of gray ostrich herl to the end of the needle. Tie four long strands of white or gray Sili Legs to the needle; the Sili Legs should be about four inches long.

Step 4

Tie a gray marabou plume onto each side of the needle. Use firm wraps of thread to secure all of the materials in place. It can be a little tricky working a knot over the rubber and feather tentacles, but secure the thread with a couple of half-hitches. The half-hitches will keep everything in place while you complete the head of the squid.

Step 5

The next step is to thread a 3-inch-long piece of pearl EZ Body tubing onto the base of the tentacles. To do this, you must remove the dubbing needle from the vise. Slip the tubing over the needle and onto the base of the marabou and other materials.

Step 6

Wrap over and squeeze the end of the EZ Body tubing against the base of the tentacles. Tie off the thread with a couple of half-hitches (this time bring the half-hitches over the dubbing needle). Clip the thread and apply a drop of fresh head cement to the knot (the cement must penetrate the tubing and bind together all of the feathers and other materials).

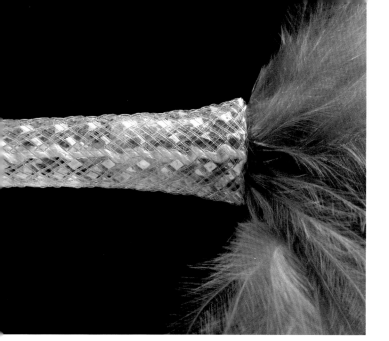

Step 7

Slip the EZ Body tubing back onto itself, forming a neat head at the base of the marabou and tentacles.

Step 8

Flatten the EZ Body tubing to create a base on which to glue the eyes (you won't be able to completely flatten the tubing). Color the top of the EZ Body tubing with a blue permanent marker; color the bottom of the tubing with a pink marker.

Step 9

Mix a small batch of five-minute epoxy. Dab a little epoxy onto each side of the head. Glue the large silver dome eyes in place.

Step 10

Place the hook in the vise. Start the thread on the hook, and tie the EZ Body tubing to the top of the hook shank. Note that the eyes hang out over the end of the hook bend. The hook, monofilament thread, and tubing are all a bit slippery; give the thread wraps a generous coat of cement to hold the head in place.

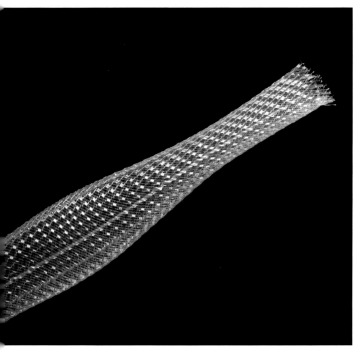

Step 11

Select a 4-inch-long piece of Flexo tubing. I am using the ½-inch-diameter tubing that contains strands of pearl Mylar tinsel; Capt. Murphy uses plain ¼-inch-diameter Flexo that is more flexible and expandable. I stroke the end of the tubing to make it narrower and easier to tie to the hook shank.

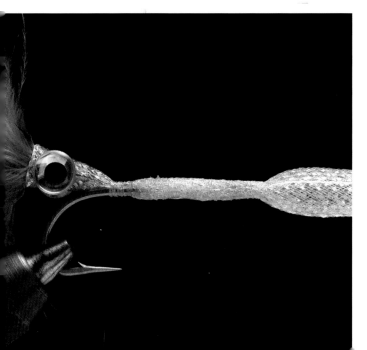

Step 12

Slip the narrowed end of the Flexo tubing onto the hook shank almost to the head of the squid. Tie off the tubing using firm wraps of thread. Coat the thread wraps with fresh head cement.

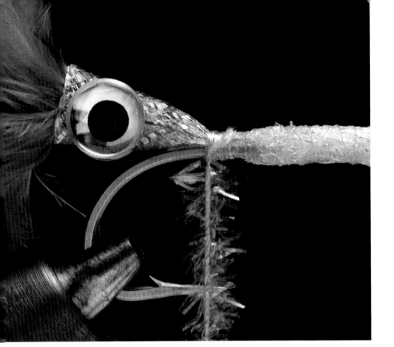

Step 13

It's time to make the underbody. Capt. Murphy uses plain pink chenille; I'm using pink Krystal Chenille. Pick a few fibers from the end of the chenille to expose the bare cotton cord. Tie the end of the cord to the hook at the base of the head. Wrap the thread up the hook to the point where you will tie off the underbody.

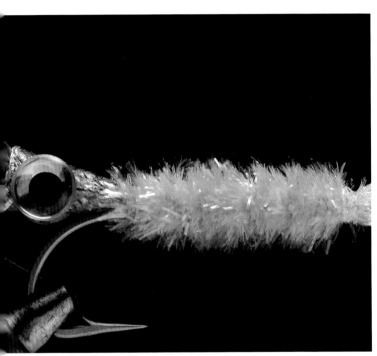

Step 14

Wrap the chenille underbody. Make firm, tightly spaced wraps of chenille. Tie off the chenille and clip the excess. Tie off the chenille with several firm half-hitches and clip. Coat the half-hitches with head cement.

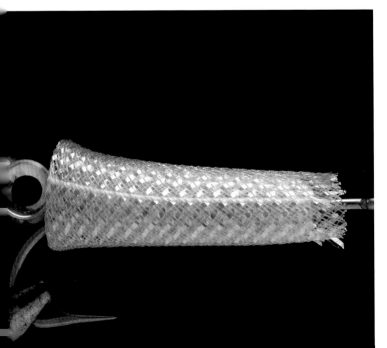

Step 15

Push the Flexo tubing back onto itself, forming the body of the fly. I suggest cutting the tubing to length, exposing a bit of bare hook shank on which to restart the thread. This is a better method than not cutting the tubing until after the body is completed; it's tough to start the thread on the large-diameter tubing, and it's also difficult to neatly trim the tough tubing after it's tied in place.

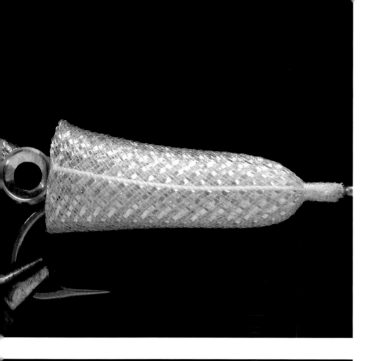

Step 16

Start the thread on the hook shank. Squeeze the end of the tubing to the shank between the thumb, index, and middle fingers of your left hand. Wrap the thread toward the end of the hook and onto the tubing; continue squeezing the tubing while wrapping the thread. Secure the tubing with very firm wraps of thread. Note that I have left plenty of room between the hook eye and the front of the body to tie on the fins and make the final thread head.

Step 17

You may color the top of the body with a blue permanent marker; color the bottom of the body with a pink marker. You may also opt not to color the body and go with the natural color of the Flexo tubing.

Step 18

Tie several strands of rainbow Krystal Flash onto each side of the body. Do not trim the Krystal Flash to length just yet.

Step 19

Tie a bunch of marabou to each side of the hook. Now is a good time to clip the Krystal Flash to length.

Step 20

Tie off and clip the thread. Color the top of the thread head with a blue permanent marker; color the bottom of the head with a pink marker. Coat the thread head with cement or epoxy. Squeeze the head and marabou to flair the fins.

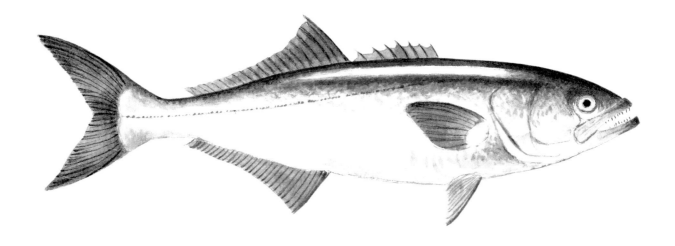

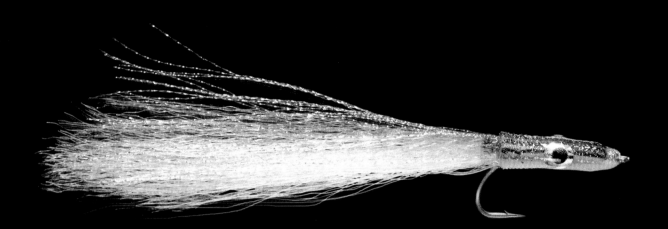

Tying the EZ Eel

I got a good lesson about the importance of using sand-eel imitations a few years ago while visiting the mouth of the Pamut River on Massachusetts's Cape Cod.

It was a warm, midafternoon June day. The tide was low and the sun was shining brightly. You couldn't ask for worse conditions when fishing for striped bass. I didn't even get my rod out of the car, but just sat on the nearby rocks while my kids played in the sand.

I had just settled down when several bait fishermen arrived. Each was armed with a spiked hoe and a 5-gallon bucket inserted in a Styrofoam life preserver. They chatted for a few minutes, and then waded out onto the calm sand flat. They soon began raking in the sand, collecting eels for their evening fishing. They would lift their hoes and deposit the sand eels in the floating buckets. It wasn't long before the seagulls gathered to scoop up the injured eels that didn't make it into the buckets. It was quite a scene.

After about half an hour, I noticed two fellows standing in the parking lot, talking and pointing toward the bait fishermen. They soon opened the trunk of their car and quickly donned waders and strung fly rods. Without saying another word, they marched into the water and waded out beyond the bait collectors. One cast—maybe two—and each was into a nice fish! The bait fishermen had stirred up the sand eels and chummed in a school of striped bass.

I ran for my fishing gear, tied on a fly I call the EZ Eel, and headed onto the flat. I caught four large schoolie striped bass that afternoon, which was quite an accomplishment given the adverse conditions. But that's the power sand eels hold over striped bass and other species of gamefish. Eels are widespread and are a part of the diets of numerous fish. You'll do well to carry a few eel patterns whenever you go fishing.

EZ Eel

Hook: Regular saltwater hook, sizes 4 to 1.

Thread: Fine clear monofilament.

Tail: Yellow and olive FisHair and strands of pearl and peacock Krystal Flash.

Head: Medium "Minnow Maker" EZ Body tubing coated with five-minute epoxy.

Eyes: Medium gold adhesive eyes.

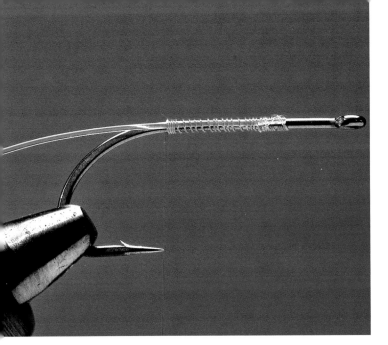

Step 1

Tie a loop of heavy monofilament at the end of the hook shank to help prevent the body materials from fouling around the hook. It's simple to do. Start the thread on the hook shank. Tie a piece of 35-pound-test monofilament on the side of the hook.

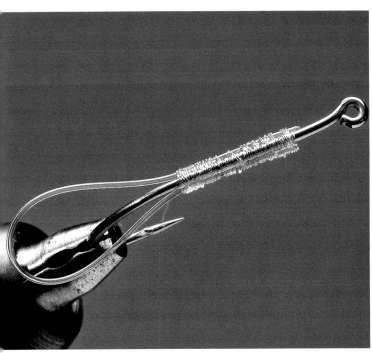

Step 2

Loop the monofilament to the other side of the hook shank and tie off. Coat the wraps of thread with head cement.

Step 3

Tie a 5- to 8-inch-long bunch of Ultra Hair to the top of the hook shank.

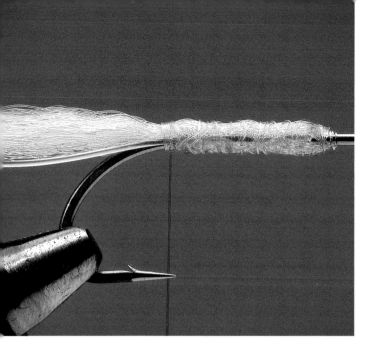

Step 4

Brush the butt ends of the Ultra Hair down the sides of the hook. Spiral wrap the thread up and down the hook, binding the ends of the Ultra Hair to the shank.

Step 5

Tie a few strands of Krystal Flash on top of the Ultra Hair.

Step 6

On this fly I have added a small bunch of olive and then a small bunch of green Ultra Hair. I have a tied a few strands of peacock Krystal Flash on top. Wrap the thread up and down the hook, tying down the butt ends of the Ultra Hair.

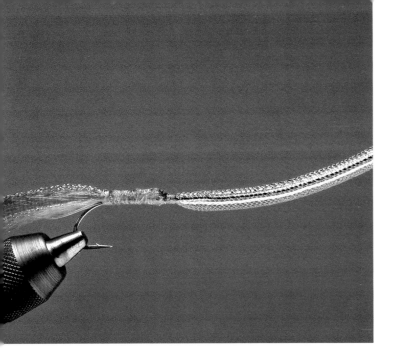

Step 7

Tie the end of a 3-inch-long piece of EZ body tubing to the end of the hook shank behind the hook eye. There are several colors of EZ Body tubing. On this fly I am using the two-tone minnow EZ Body. Tie off the thread using several half-hitches and clip. Coat the half-hitches with head cement.

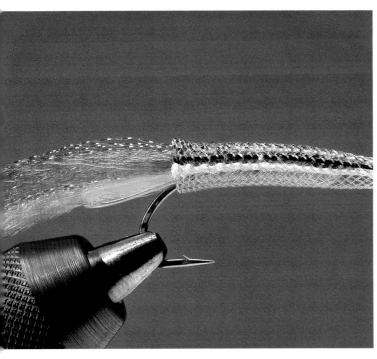

Step 8

Push the EZ Body tubing back on itself to form a bullet-shaped head.

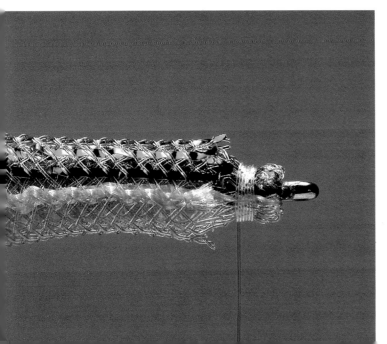

Step 9

Push the outer layer of tubing back to expose the inner layer. Restart the thread on the hook shank or the inner layer of tubing.

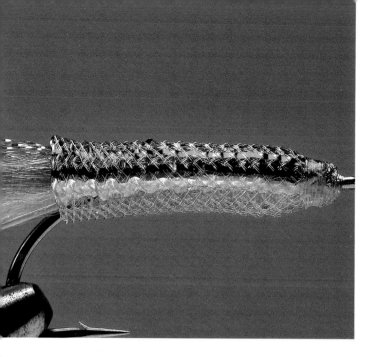

Step 10

Push the outer layer of tubing forward to the thread. Tie off the end of the outer layer. Make a neat thread head, tie off, and clip. Place a drop of head cement on the thread knot; monofilament thread is very slick, and the cement will hold everything in place until you coat the head with epoxy.

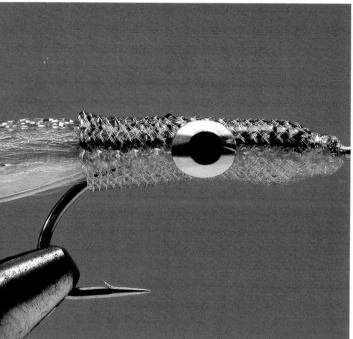

Step 11

Place a large adhesive eye on each side of the head.

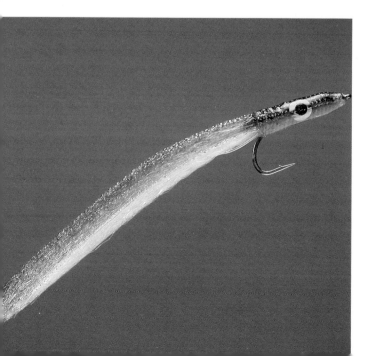

Step 12

Coat the head and eyes with five-minute epoxy. The EZ Eel is a very durable, effective pattern.

chapter 5 guide flies

Trashline Squid
tied by Capt. Tom McQuade
St. John, Virgin Islands

The Trashline Squid demonstrates the effective use of adding a small glass rattle to a fly. When the fly is slowly stripped through the water, the small beads slap around inside of the rattle, giving off fish-enticing vibrations. Small rattles could be added to a wide range of patterns. Capt. McQuade uses this fly in the evenings for snook, tarpon, and a variety of offshore species.

Hook: Regular saltwater hook, size 2/0.
Thread: White, size 6/0.
Weed guard: 30-pound-test fluorocarbon.
Feelers & head: White calftail, Angel Hair, and pearl Krystal Flash.
Body: Pearl Mylar tubing on the hook shank and a small glass rattle coated with epoxy.
Eyes: Medium silver adhesive eyes.

Banded Shrimp
tied by Capt. Tom McQuade
St. John, Virgin Islands

The Banded Shrimp is a good pattern for fishing the flats. Capt. McQuade tied this fly for catching bonefish, snapper, and sea trout. He ties the Banded Shrimp in white, tan, pink, and olive.

Hook: Regular saltwater hook, sizes 6 and 4.
Thread: Color to match the body, size 6/0.
Weed guard: 20-pound-test monofilament.
Head & antennae: Calftail and pearl Krystal Flash.
Claws: Ginger neck hackle tipped with a black permanent marker.
Eyes: Melted monofilament.
Body: Thread with a rib of pearl Krystal Flash.
Legs: Grizzly hackle clipped on top.
Shell: Tan grizzly hackle banded with a black permanent marker and coated with epoxy.

Fuzzy Shrimp
tied by Capt. Tom McQuade
St. John, Virgin Islands

This is another of Capt. McQuade's original patterns. The Fuzzy Shrimp is a great fly to have when the bonefish come up on the flats. Even a tier of modest accomplishments will quickly master this fly. Tie the Fuzzy Shrimp in tan, pink, and olive.

Hook: Regular saltwater hook, sizes 6 and 4.
Thread: Color to match the body, size 6/0.
Weed guard: 20-pound-test monofilament.
Head: Calftail.
Claws: Barred ginger neck hackles.
Eyes: Melted monofilament.
Body & legs: Neck hackles wound up the hook shank. Clip the fibers close on the top and sides of the fly.

Epoxy Sand Eel
tied by Capt. James Ellis
West Barnstable, Massachusetts

Capt. Ellis is a real fan of circle hooks. He believes they hook more fish, and that the fish are easier to release. The Epoxy Sand Eel, one of Capt. Ellis's own patterns, is tied on a Daiichi circle hook. The Epoxy Sand Eel is the perfect pattern for casting to striped bass, bluefish, and other gamefish along the northeast Atlantic Coast.

Hook: Daiichi 3847, size 1.
Thread: White, size 6/0.
Tail: Light olive and white bucktail with strands of pearl Flashabou.
Body: Pearl Bill's Bodi Braid coated with five-minute epoxy.
Eyes: Small gold adhesive eyes.

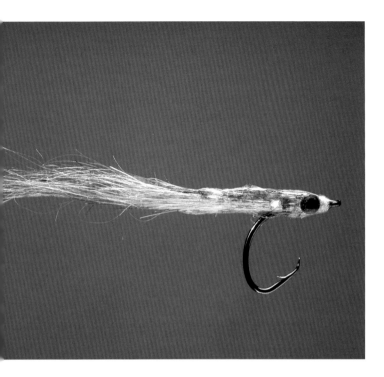

Sand Eel
tied by Capt. James Ellis
West Barnstable, Massachusetts

Here's another of Capt. Ellis's favorite sand-eel imitations. Whereas the tail on his Epoxy Sand Eel is tied out of bucktail, the tail on the basic Sand Eel is all synthetic materials. Although the Sand Eel is tied to imitate a real eel, the fly will do an admirable job of matching a variety of small baitfish.

Hook: Daiichi 3847, size 1.
Thread: White, size 6/0.
Tail: Pearl and gold Angel Hair stiffened near the hook with a light coat of Softex.
Gills: Red permanent marker.
Eyes: Small gold adhesive eyes.
Body: Coat the tail fibers lying along the hook shank with epoxy.

Bugger Shrimp
tied by Bob Lindquist
East Patchoque, New York

The Bugger Shrimp is tied using a long dubbing loop made out of stainless-steel wire. There are several machines on the market designed for creating large dubbing loops, which are sometimes referred to as dubbing brushes. Making a dubbing brush is simple. The fur is inserted into the loop and the loop is spun closed (the entire spun dubbing brush can be up to ten inches long and used to tied several flies). Next, one end of the dubbing brush is tied to the end of the hook shank. The thread is wrapped up the shank, followed by the dubbing brush. Tie off the brush and clip the excess. Bob ties this fly in tan, light olive, rootbeer, and pink.

Hook: Gamakatsu SS15 or SL11-3L3H, sizes 6 to 2.
Thread: Flat-waxed nylon to match the body.
Tail: Llama mixed with Angel Hair.
Eyes: Melted monofilament.
Body: Llama and a fine flash material spun into a dubbing brush.

RM Sting
tied by Richard Murphy
Georgetown, Massachusetts

Richard Murphy is one of the ablest guides on the northern East Coast. One of his experiences included working with scientists studying striped bass. "I had the opportunity to work with the University of Massachusetts Striped Bass Dietary Inventory Project," says Murphy. "My job was to accompany a couple of biologists to specific locations within the Essex River estuary system. I'd catch and hand the bass to the biologists who'd anaesthetize the fish, pump their stomachs, and then revive and release the fish. Overwhelmingly, the stripers' stomachs contained grass shrimp and immature crabs." The Sting is a great imitation of a grass shrimp.

Hook: Eagle Claw 413 jig hook, size 2.
Thread: Fine monofilament.
Antennae: Four to seven strands of black Krystal Flash.
Weight: Medium dumbbell eyes.
Eyes: Medium Nymph Eyes (or melted monofilament).
Legs & claws: Grizzly neck hackle.
Shell: Tan 1/16-inch-thick Live Body foam.

RM Soft Short
tied by Richard Murphy
Georgetown, Massachusetts

Lobster fishermen always tell stories about catching striped bass in their traps; the fish poke their way into the entrances to get at the delectable crustaceans. Murphy's RM Soft Short "is an impressionistic imitation of a molting juvenile American lobster." This is another advanced pattern for the more accomplished tiers.

Hook: TMC 911S, size 3/0.
Thread: Fine monofilament.
Eyes: Black Live Body foam.
Antennae & head: Old orange floating fly line and olive bucktail.
Claws: Dark olive pheasant body feathers inserted into small clear EZ Body tubing.
Weight: Large dumbbell eyes.
Rattle: Large glass rattle inserted into a piece of small clear EZ Body tubing and tied to the hook shank between the claws and the dumbbell eyes.
Body: Grizzly hackle Palmer-wrapped up the hook and colored with permanent markers.

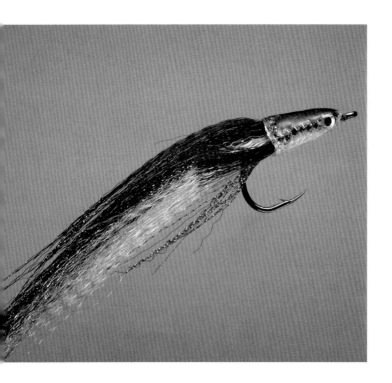

RM American Eel
tied by Richard Murphy
Georgetown, Massachusetts

Although the RM American Eel is a large fly—it measures close to ten inches long—it is surprisingly light. It's a good pattern to have when fishing for striped bass and bluefish in the Northeast. Although it appears complicated, careful beginners should be able to create a credible American Eel.

Hook: TMC 600SP, size 2/0.
Thread: Fine monofilament.
Tail: Black Ultra Hair, tan ultraviolet Krystal Hair, polar bear Ultra Hair, and red Krystal Flash. Add a drop of superglue to the base of the tail and squeeze the materials.
Fins: Black Ultra Hair.
Head: Large pearl EZ Body tubing coated with epoxy.
Eyes: Small silver adhesive eyes.

Soda Straw Shrimp
tied by Capt. Ron Kowalyk
Ft. Myers, Florida

Capt. Kowalyk doesn't limit his tying to using the ordinary materials found in the local fly shop. His Soda Straw Shrimp is made with, you guessed it, a plastic soda straw. This clear straw allows the underlying body materials to show through, but you can also use a pink or orange straw. Another idea is to use the ridged section of a flexible straw to give the pattern a segmented appearance similar to the shell back of a shrimp. After tying the materials to the hook, cut a length of straw as shown in the photo. Split the straw along the bottom (opposite the pointed head). Slip the straw over the top of the fly and secure with firm wraps of thread.

Hook: Mustad 3407, sizes 2 to 1/0.
Thread: Brown flat-waxed nylon.
Antennae: Orange bucktail and gold or copper Flashabou.
Eyes: Black plastic or melted monofilament.
Body: Brown Cactus Chenille.
Legs & head: Grizzly hackle Palmer-wrapped over the chenille body.

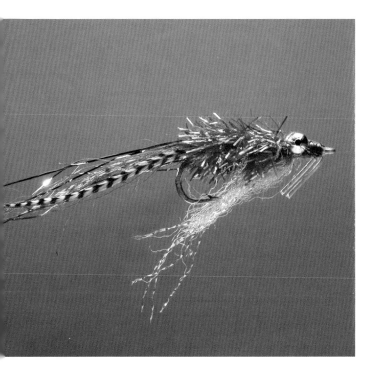

Cinnamon Cactus Chenille Shrimp
tied by Capt. Ron Kowalyk
Ft. Myers, Florida

*Here's a more basic shrimp imitation that novice tiers
will love. The soft materials give the Cactus Chenille
Shrimp a lot of fish-enticing motion. This pattern will
work everywhere shrimp are a part of the gamefish diet.*

Hook: Mustad 3407, sizes 2 to 1/0.
Weed guard: 30-pound-test monofilament.
Thread: Brown flat-waxed nylon.
Antennae: Brown bucktail, copper Flashabou, and
grizzly hackle tied on each side.
Body: Brown Cactus Chenille.
Throat: Tan synthetic hair such as Poly Bear and
strands of pearl Krystal Flash.
Eyes: Depending upon how deep you will fish the fly,
choose from melted monofilament, large bead-chain,
or medium lead dumbbell.

Mega Shrimp
tied by Pat Ford
Miami, Florida

*Pat isn't a guide, but he is an inventive fly tier and
one hell of a fisherman. He travels around the world
in search of good sport, and has plenty of good stories
to share about his adventures. The photo on his business
card shows Pat feeding a large barracuda by holding
a piece of fish in his mouth! His Mega Shrimp will
attract fish, too.*

Hook: Regular saltwater hook, sizes 2 to 1/0.
Thread: Orange flat-waxed nylon.
Eyes: Large lead dumbbell eyes painted yellow
and black.
Tail: Brown marabou, grizzly hackles, and strands
of rainbow Krystal Flash.
Body: Tan chenille.
Legs: Grizzly hackle Palmer-wrapped over the body.

Mega Shrimp 2
tied by Pat Ford
Miami, Florida

*The companion pattern to Pat Ford's Mega Shrimp.
He uses these flies to catch Florida bonefish and permit,
especially during the winter months.*

Hook: Regular saltwater hook, sizes 2 to 1/0.
Thread: Orange flat-waxed nylon.
Eyes: Large lead dumbbell eyes painted yellow
and black.
Tail: Brown marabou, grizzly hackles, and strands
of rainbow Krystal Flash.
Body: Orange chenille.
Legs: Grizzly hackle Palmer-wrapped over the body.

Reggie's Bubble Shrimp
tied by Richard "Reggie" Regensburg
Ocean View, New Jersey

*I first met Reggie at the annual International Fly
Tying Symposium. While he is not a guide, he is
nonetheless an incredibly inventive fly tier. Reggie
does amazing things with materials that were never
designed for tying flies.*

Hook: Mustad 34007, your choice of size.
Thread: Clear monofilament.
Antennae: Olive and pearl Krystal Flash.
Eyes: Melted monofilament.
Body: Bubble pack clipped to shape and threaded
onto the hook.
Back: Strands of pearl and olive Krystal Flash, tied
on at the hook bend. Fold the Krystal Flash over the
top of the body and tie off behind the hook eye.
Legs: Gray or olive saddle hackle Palmer-wrapped
over the body and clipped on top.
Shell back: Clear caulking (coat the antennae and
back of the fly, and form a shrimp tail over the
hook eye).

Lenny's Tarpon Shrimp
tied by Capt. Lenny Moffo
Big Pine Key, Florida

Capt. Moffo uses this pattern mostly to catch tarpon, but it also works on cobia, permit, and other species that feed on large shrimp.

Hook: Regular saltwater hook, size 3/0.
Thread: Tan Monocord.
Antennae & head: Brown Poly Bear, brown Krystal Flash, two tan and two dark tan grizzly hackles.
Eyes: 80-pound-test monofilament. Place a bead of epoxy on the end of the monofilament to make an eye. Paint the eye with chartreuse lacquer.
Collar: Large ginger hackle.

Jumpin' Shrimp
tied by Capt. Lenny Moffo
Big Pine Key, Florida

"When the shrimp come to the top of the water, we call it a shrimp hatch," says Capt. Moffo. The shrimp actually jump up out of the water when they are being driven to the surface by gamefish. This usually occurs in the early morning, and the seagulls are the tip-off. The depth of the water will usually be between two and eight feet. The Jumpin' Shrimp is not weighted so it will remain near the surface and imitate a real shrimp."

Hook: Regular saltwater hook, size 1/0.
Thread: Tan Monocord.
Antennae & head: Tan Poly Bear (use a brown permanent marker to add dark bars), brown Krystal Flash, and mallard flank fibers.
Eyes: 50-pound-test monofilament. Place a bead of epoxy on the end of the monofilament to make an eye. Paint the eye with brown lacquer.
Body: Tan Poly Bear wrapped up the hook shank.
Legs: Two dark tan hackles Palmer wrapped over the body.
Shell back: Tan Poly Bear.

chapter 6

Flats Flies That Catch Fish

INNOVATIVE FLIES FOR CATCHING PRIZED GAMEFISH

Wading the flats is a favorite way to fish the salt; the water is warm, the sun is bright, and an angler never knows when a trophy fish will ghost its way onto the flats. The Florida Keys, one of our most popular fishing destinations, contains thousands of miles of flats featuring prized bonefish, permit, and other species of fish. The Texas coast is overlooked by many anglers, but it features excellent opportunities to cast to redfish. The entire Caribbean and several Central American countries offer excellent flats fishing. Whether you fish from a flats skiff or prefer wading, you must have the correct flies.

Flats flies share several characteristics; understand these features and you'll be able to develop your own successful flats patterns. First, most effective flats flies imitate some form of food that is found on the sand and marl flats, usually small shrimp, crabs or other crustaceans. Some patterns closely match a common flats forage, but others are general representations. Here's where you'll find real differences between the various guides and tiers: some insist that successful patterns match the colors of the natural food (the local forage often match the color of the sand, coral or marl bottom), while other guides select patterns dressed in colors that stand out against the ocean floor.

Second, most flats flies are tied "weedless." Many flies are designed to ride with their hooks pointing up, usually by placing weighted dumbbell eyes on top of the shanks to force the hooks to turn over when fishing. This is especially important when fishing something like a crab pattern that you might wish to occasionally sink to the bottom; a fly with the hook facing up is less likely to catch grass or snag on coral.

Other tiers create weed guards out of monofila-

ment. Examine the guides's flies at the end of this chapter and you'll see many flies incorporating one or both of these important features.

Flats flies generally run on the small side. About the largest patterns are tied on size 1 hooks, and many are tied down to size 8. The forage we are imitating are fairly small, and the flies are, too.

Finally, and this is just a personal opinion, flats flies are among the most inventive patterns in fly tying. With a bit of fur, feathers, and a few synthetic materials, we can create realistic imitations of crabs and other crustaceans. These flies are fun to tie and fun to fish. I can only occasionally visit the flats, but I do enjoy tying the flies; they make me feel so much closer to those tropical climes when the snow is beating against the window and piling up at the door.

I've selected two crab patterns to tie for this chapter. The first is a fly called the Critter Crab, a simple impressionistic pattern that takes its share of redfish, bonefish, and other flats species. This fly was submitted to me by Capt. Christopher Dean of Miami, Florida, and is identical to Capt. Tim Borski's Bonefish Critter.

The second pattern we will tie was designed by Capt. Russ Shirley of St. Petersburg, Florida. Capt. Shirley's Rockin' Crab is fun to make and has a neat rocking movement when resting still. It's a unique fly that you'll want to add to your flats fly box.

This chapter also contains a large number of guides's flies. The guides living in Florida and the Caribbean sent a lot of patterns, but several guides living in the Northeast sent copies of the patterns they use when fishing in the South. What can I say? Everyone loves fishing the flats.

The Critter Crab

There are several excellent crab patterns that have bodies made out of rug yarn. Aunt Lydia's Rug Yarn is the most popular, but there are other brands on the market. All of these yarns are tough and stiff, and can be used to make convincing crab imitations. Regular yarn used for making sweaters and other clothing items is no substitute for rug yarn—at least for tying crab flies.

I should point out that it's getting tougher to find stores that carry rug yarn. One owner of a local crafts store says that the boom in latch-hook rug making is over, and that few students sign up for the classes on rug making held at his store. As a result, he and other stores are reducing or eliminating their inventories of rug-making supplies. Look for packages of pre-cut rug-making yarn at larger crafts stores, and purchase several packages in tan, brown, and olive. You'll be able to tie dozens of flies from only a few packages of yarn.

The Critter Crab is a simple pattern to tie. By changing the color of the yarn, or by coloring the finished flies with a permanent marker, you'll be able to create crab flies that match the real crustaceans wherever you fish.

Critter Crab

Hook: Regular saltwater hook, size 4.

Thread: White, size A

Weight: Small dumbbell eyes.

Head: Orange Crystal Chenille.

Eyes: Melted 25-pound-test monofilament.

Antennae: Brown hackle.

Body: Gold or tan rug yarn colored with an olive permanent marker.

Weed guard: 25-pound-test monofilament.

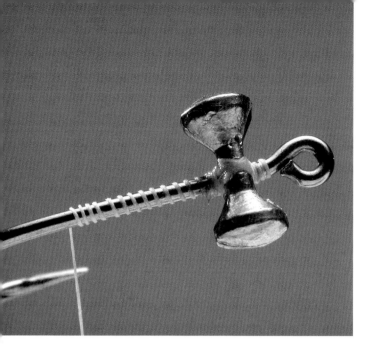

Step 1

Start the thread near the front of the hook shank. Tie on the dumbbell eyes with a series of figure-eight wraps of thread.

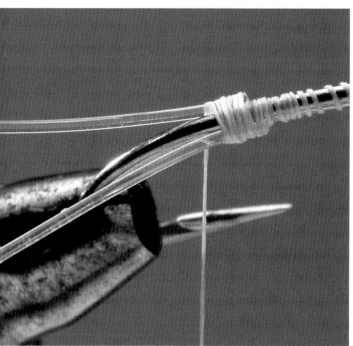

Step 2

Wrap the thread to the end of the hook shank. Tie on a pair of melted monofilament eyes.

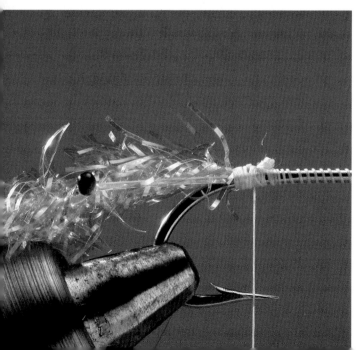

Step 3

Tie on a piece of orange Crystal Chenille between the monofilament eyes. The chenille will add a dash of fish-attracting flash to the fly.

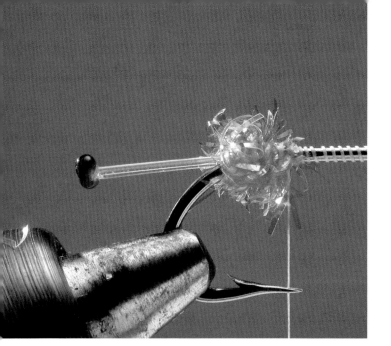

Step 4
Wrap the chenille around the base of the eyes. Tie off and clip the excess chenille.

Step 5
Tie on and wrap a brown saddle hackle around the base of the chenille head. The hackle fibers will pulsate when the fly is stripped through the water.

Step 6
Tie the first piece of rug yarn tight against the base of the wrapped hackle. Secure the yarn to the hook shank with two firm figure-eight wraps.

Step 7

Continue working up the hook shank, tying on strands of rug yarn as you go. Five pieces of yarn is enough to cover the shank of a size 4 hook. After tying on the last piece of yarn, tie off and clip the thread. Place a drop of head cement down the center of the yarn body.

Step 8

Clip the yarn to create the rounded shape of a crab. Work slowly and make several small cuts.

Step 9

Use a fine comb to brush out the strands of yarn.

Step 10

If you'd like a darker crab, just color the top of the body with a permanent marker. In this case I've used an olive marker.

Step 11

Re-start the thread in front of the dumbbell eyes. Tie on a monofilament weed guard.

Step 12

The Critter Crab is an impressionistic pattern that even a novice can tie. The materials are inexpensive and durable, and you can make this fly in several colors.

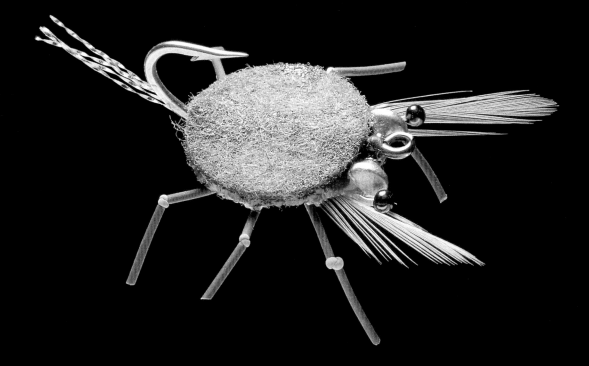

The Rockin Crab

It's really not accurate to say that you tie the Rockin' Crab. That's because you'll use more construction than tying techniques for crafting this pattern. Aside from tying on the dumbbell eyes and tail, everything else is glued to the fly. Is this a big deal? I don't think so; it's a very efficient way to work, and epoxy creates a very durable pattern.

There are a lot of crab patterns, but I selected the Rockin' Crab for two reasons. First, every angler should carry a smattering of crab flies when fishing the flats. The Rockin' Crab, which can be tied in a variety of colors, is fairly realistic and easy to make. Second, as the name implies, the Rockin' Crab has a neat rocking motion when twitched along the bottom. This movement mimics the standing and walking movement of a real crab. Do the fish get the idea? I don't know, but it's very inventive and I think you'll want to make at least a couple of Rockin' Crabs.

The body of the Rockin' Crab is made out of two round adhesive-backed felt pads. These pre-cut pads come in brown and tan, and one package often contains pads in a couple of crablike sizes. Capt. Shirley used brown pads on the sample fly he sent to me, so I selected the same material. You might want to use tan felt pads for making crabs for fishing primarily over sand flats, and you can color the tan pads with an olive permanent marker to create olive Rockin' Crabs.

Rockin Crab

Hook: Regular saltwater hook, sizes 4 and 2.

Thread: Size A, color to match the felt body.

Eyes: Small dumbbell eyes.

Tail: Strand of Krystal Flash.

Body: Two round adhesive-backed felt pads.

Eyes: Melted 25-pound-test clear monofilament.

Legs: Six strands of rubber legs, color to match the body. Tie a knot in the middle of each strand to create the leg joints.

Claws: Two hackles, color to match the body.

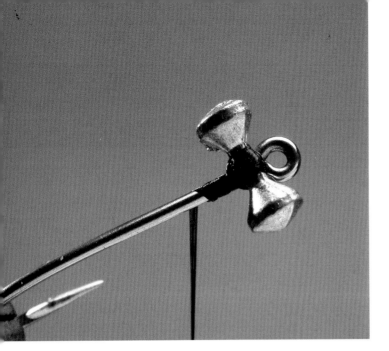

Step 1

Start the thread near the hook eye. Lay a base of thread on the hook shank. Tie a set of small dumbbell eyes to the top of the shank next to the hook eye. This weight forces the fly to ride hook-point-up when fishing the fly.

Step 2

Wrap a thick, even base of thread on the hook shank. This thread gives the epoxy something to bind to when gluing the body to the hook. Tie a few strands of Krystal Flash to the hook. Tie off and clip the thread.

Step 3

Mix a small dab of epoxy. Spread a little epoxy along the thread base on the hook shank. Place one felt pad on the bottom of the hook (adhesive side up). Smear epoxy on the adhesive side of the pad, and place a second pad (adhesive side down) on top. Press the two pads together. Allow the epoxy to harden before proceeding.

Step 4

Mix another dab of epoxy. Add a drop of enamel hobby paint to the epoxy (select a color that matches the felt body). Apply the epoxy to the side of the body facing up in the vise (this will be the bottom of the completed fly). Stick the two monofilament eyes, two hackle pinchers, and six rubber legs in the epoxy.

Step 5

As the epoxy thickens, turn the fly over in the vise so the glue is on the bottom (the crab is now in the finished position). The epoxy should sag and form a rounded belly on the fly. The Rockin' Crab will rock back and forth on this round bottom.

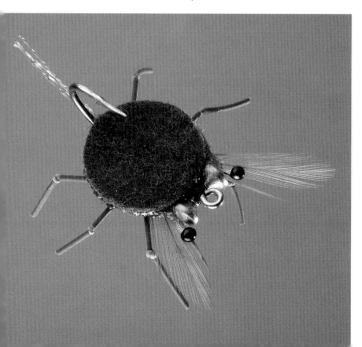

Step 6

The Rockin' Crab requires more construction than tying techniques, but it's a valuable pattern to have when fishing for permit, bonefish, and other crab-eating flats gamefish.

Rootbeer Sugarloaf Special
tied by Capt. Dexter Simmons
Key West, Florida

The Sugarloaf Special series of flies are designed to catch bonefish, permit, and other species of fish that visit the Florida flats. The dumbbell eyes, tied on the top of the shank, force the fly to ride hook-point-up, and the monofilament snag guard contributes to making the pattern a good choice where weeds are a problem.

Hook: Regular saltwater hook, sizes 8 and 6.
Thread: Black 3/0.
Eyes: Small lead dumbbell painted dark red with black pupils.
Tail: Two furnace hackles and strands of pearl Krystal Flash.
Body: Brown Crystal Chenille.
Hackle: Brown.
Weed guard: 40-pound-test monofilament.

Olive Sugarloaf Special
tied by Capt. Dexter Simmons
Key West, Florida

A cousin to the Rootbeer Sugarloaf Special, this olive pattern gives you an alternative when the brown version fails.

Hook: Regular saltwater hook, sizes 8 and 6.
Thread: Black 3/0.
Eyes: Small lead dumbbell painted yellow with black pupils.
Tail: Two grizzly hackles dyed yellow and two or three strands of peacock herl.
Body: Yellow Crystal Chenille.
Hackle: Olive.
Weed guard: 40-pound-test monofilament.

Critter Crab
tied by Capt. Chris Dean
Miami, Florida

"This fly was designed by Tim Borski," says Capt. Dean. "I started tying it in 1993 after seeing one of Tim's original patterns. I thought it was tied with rug yarn like a Merkin Crab, but since then every reference I've seen for it specifies ram's wool. The rug yarn works great so I've stayed with it. This is my favorite fly for catching tailing bonefish."

Hook: Mustad 34007, size 4.
Thread: White flat-waxed nylon.
Butt: Light orange sparkle chenille.
Eyes: Melted 25-pound-test monofilament.
Hackle: Two wraps of brown hackle.
Body: Five pieces of yellow or tan Aunt Lydia's Rug Yarn tied on the bottom of the hook and combed out to blend the fibers. Clip the body to shape and coat the center line of the fly with head cement. Color the top of the fly (facing the hook point) with an olive marker.
Eyes: Extra-small lead dumbbell eyes.
Weed guard: 16-pound-test monofilament.

Dean Permit Crab
tied by Capt. Chris Dean
Miami, Florida

"I created this fly is 1980. I like to use it for cruising permit. The fly has a neutral buoyancy and doesn't drop to the bottom like other weighted flies."

Hook: Mustad 34007, size 1/0.
Thread: Brown 3/0.
Eyes: Large silver bead-chain.
Claws: Two brown hackles tied on each side and curving out. Spin and clip short a small bunch of deer hair behind the eyes before tying on the feathers; this small bunch of deer hair will help spread the claws.
Body: Natural brown deer hair, spun and clipped flat on the top and bottom. Clip the edges of the body to form the shape of a small crab.

Emery Epoxy Fly
tied by Capt. Chris Dean
Miami, Florida

This is one of Capt. Dean's favorite redfish flies. He says that he gets strikes with this pattern when all others fail.

Hook: Mustad 34007, size 1.
Thread: Red flat-waxed nylon.
Tail: Three white saddle hackles tied on each side and splayed out, and strands of pearl Flashabou.
Hackle: Red saddle hackle.
Eyes: Melted 100-pound-test monofilment tied in the middle of the hook shank.
Body: Fasco two-part paste epoxy. Apply the epoxy to form a diamond-shaped body.
Weed guard: 16-pound-test monofilament.

The Other Crab
tied by Capt. Tom McQuade
St. John, Virgin Islands

Capt. McQuade ties a large number of very creative patterns and tests them in some of the best bonefish and permit waters in the world. His Other Crab is tied almost entirely out of barred ginger hackles.

Hook: Regular saltwater hook, size 2.
Thread: Tan 6/0.
Eyes: Melted monofilament.
Body: Barred ginger hackle Palmer-wrapped up the hook shank (you may add weight to the fly by first adding a few wraps of lead wire to the shank). Clip the hackle fibers from the top, front, and bottom of the fly (leave the fibers on the side of the fly opposite the monofilament eyes). Clip the remaining fibers to form the shape of the crab. Coat the top of the body with Softex.
Legs & claws: Barred ginger hackle placed in the fresh Softex. Color the tips of the legs and claws with a black permanent marker.
Weed guard: 30-pound-test monofilament.

Tan E-Z Crab
tied by Capt. Tom McQuade
St. John, Virgin Islands

The E-Z Crab is one of Capt. McQuade's patterns designed for catching bonefish.

Hook: Regular saltwater hook, sizes 6 and 4.
Thread: Clear monofilament.
Eyes: Black beads glued on monofilament stems.
Legs & claws: Barred ginger hackle.
Body: Tan E-Z Shape Sparkle Body. Sparkle Body is a thick, non-running waterproof adhesive.
Weed guard: 20-pound-test monofilament.

Pink Imitator Shrimp
tied by Capt. Tom McQuade
St. John, Virgin Islands

The Imitator Shrimp series of flies are great for catching small tarpon, bonefish, snapper, and barracuda. The small glass rattle gives off a small commotion that helps the fish find the fly.

Hook: Regular saltwater hook, size 2.
Thread: Pink 3/0.
Tail: A small tuft of white calf's tail hair, two strands of pearl Krystal Flash, and two barred ginger hackles.
Eyes: Plastic monofilament eyes.
Body: Pink thread wrapped up the hook shank and a rib of pearl Krystal Flash.
Rattle: Small glass rattle epoxied to the body (coat both the rattle and body with epoxy).
Weed guard: 30-pound-test monofilament.

chapter 6 guide flies

Pearl Imitator Shrimp
tied by Capt. Tom McQuade
St. John, Virgin Islands

Hook: Regular saltwater hook, size 2.
Thread: White 3/0.
Tail: A small tuft of white calf's tail hair, two strands of pearl Krystal Flash, and two barred ginger hackles.
Eyes: Plastic monofilament eyes.
Body: Narrow pearl Mylar tubing.
Rattle: Small glass rattle epoxied to the Mylar body (coat both the rattle and Mylar tubing with epoxy).
Weed guard: 30-pound-test monofilament.

The Thing
tied by Capt. Tom McQuade
St. John, Virgin Islands

The Thing is a general crustacean imitation that mimics several small creatures inhabiting the flats around the Virgin Islands. It's a good pattern for catching bonefish, sea trout, permit, and snappers.

Hook: Regular saltwater hook, sizes 8 to 4.
Thread: Clear monofilament.
Head & antennae: A small tuft of white calf's tail hair and two strands of black Krystal Flash.
Legs: Grizzly Sili Legs.
Eyes: Extra small plastic monofilament eyes.
Body: Grizzly hackle Palmer-wrapped up the hook shank and clipped to shape.
Weed guard: 30-pound-test monofilament.

The Other Thing (Dark Tan)
tied by Capt. Tom McQuade
St. John, Virgin Islands

Capt. McQuade says that the flats surrounding the Virgin Island host a variety of small crustaceans. The Other Thing is a series of inventive patterns designed to imitate these crustaceans.

Hook: Regular saltwater hook, sizes 8 to 4.
Thread: Clear monofilament.
Head & claws A small tuft of white calf's tail hair and two barred ginger hackles. Color the tips of the hackles with a black permanent marker.
Eyes: Extra small plastic monofilament eyes.
Body: Dark-tan barred grizzly hackle Palmer-wrapped up the hook shank and clipped to shape. Coat the top of the body with Softex.
Weed guard: 30-pound-test monofilament.

The Other Thing (Light Tan)
tied by Capt. Tom McQuade
St. John, Virgin Islands

Hook: Regular saltwater hook, sizes 8 to 4.
Thread: Clear monofilament.
Head & claws: A small tuft of white calf's tail hair and two barred ginger hackles.
Eyes: Extra small plastic monofilament eyes.
Body: Light-tan barred grizzly hackle Palmer-wrapped up the hook shank and clipped to shape. Coat the top of the body with Softex.
Weed guard: 30-pound-test monofilament.

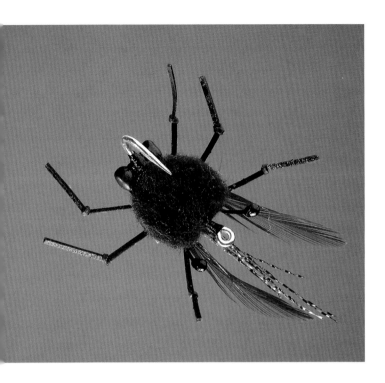

The Rockin' Crab
tied by Capt. Russ Shirley
St. Petersburg, Florida

The Rockin' Crab is tied with a hard, rounded bottom that allows the fly to actually rock back and forth. I placed Capt. Shirley's fly on both hard and soft surfaces, and it rocked and moved like a real crab. Capt. Shirley uses his realistic Rockin' Crab to catch redfish when sight-fishing over hard or soft bottoms. Note that the eyes, antennae, claws, and legs are glued to the bottom of the body.

Hook: Regular saltwater hook, sizes 6 and 4.
Thread: Black flat-waxed nylon.
Lead eyes: Small dumbbell eyes.
Body: Brown adhesive felt pads (one pad is placed on each side of the fly and clipped to shape). Coat the bottom of the body with 30-minute epoxy mixed with black hobby enamel. Place the eyes, antennae, claws, and legs in the wet epoxy.
Eyes: Melted monofilament.
Antennae: Black and rootbeer Krystal Flash.
Claws: Brown hackle tips.
Legs: Sili Legs (black with red flecks).

Permit Snack
tied by Carter Andrews
Crooked Island, Bahamas

Hook: Regular saltwater hook, size 6.
Thread: Pink 6/0.
Eyes: Small silver dumbbells.
Antennae & head: Strands of pearl Krystal Flash, and very small tufts of white Fly Fur and orange marabou.
Eyes: Melted 25-pound-test monofilament.
Body: Pearl Mylar braid.
Wing: Tufts of tan rabbit fur.

MOG Crab

tied by Capt. Ron Kowalyk
Ft. Myers, Florida

The MOG (Mother of Glue) Crab is the perfect fly for casting to redfish, black drum, and pompano.

Hook: Regular saltwater hook, sizes 2 to 1/0.
Thread: Brown 3/0.
Eyes: Large silver bead-chain.
Tail: Copper Flashabou and Live Rubber legs (yellow and black).
Hackle: Grizzly.
Head: Hot glue.
Weed guard: 60-pound-test monofilament.

Everything Fly

tied by Capt. Len Roberts
Islamorada, Florida

The Everything Fly does it all. It catches bonefish, permit, snook, barracuda, tarpon, and all of the other species swimming the Florida flats. You'll want to carry a few Everything Flies the next time you visit the Keys.

Hook: Mustad 34011, sizes 4 to 1/0.
Thread: Clear monofilament.
Tail: Strands of rainbow Krystal Flash and a bunch of tan Fly Fur. Tie a cree hackle tip to each side of the tail.
Hackle: Cree, Palmer-wrapped halfway up the hook shank.
Eyes: Small lead dumbbell eyes.
Weed guard: 20-pound-test monofilament.

Lenny's Blenny
tied by Capt. Len Roberts
Islamorada, Florida

Capt. Roberts spends much of his time guiding for permit and bonefish on the flats near his home in Islamorada. Lenny's Blenny, one of his favorite patterns, has accounted for many big fish.

Hook: Mustad 34007, sizes 4 and 2.
Thread: Clear monofilament.
Tail: Rainbow Krystal Flash and tan marabou.
Body: Spun deer hair clipped to form a rounded, shaggy body.
Hackle: Grizzly (natural or dyed olive) Palmer wrapped through the body.
Eyes: Small lead dumbbell eyes.
Weed guard: 20-pound-test monofilament.
Head: Five-minute epoxy.

Len's False Pichard
tied by Capt. Len Roberts
Islamorada, Florida

This is another of Capt. Roberts's patterns that catches a variety of gamefish: bonefish, sea trout, redfish, and cobia.

Hook: Mustad 34007, sizes 1 to 2/0.
Thread: Clear monofilament.
Tail: Strands of pearl Flashabou and six white saddle hackles. Tie a natural grizzly hackle on each side of the tail.
Hackle: Red, tied at the back of the body.
Body: Pearl Crystal Chenille.
Eyes: Large silver bead-chain.
Weed guard: 20-pound-test monofilament.

Bristle Worm
tied by Tim Borski
Islamorada, Florida

The Bristle Worm is one of Tim Borski's favorite patterns to cast to tailing bonefish.

Hook: Regular saltwater hook, sizes 4 or 2.
Thread: White flat-waxed nylon.
Tail: Tan craft fur barred with a brown permanent marker and a couple of strands of copper Flashabou.
Hackle: Grizzly hackle.
Eyes: Medium silver bead-chain.
Head: Shaggy olive dubbing
Weed guard: 20-pound-test monofilament.

Chernobyl Crab
tied by Tim Borski
Islamorada, Florida

The Chernobyl Crab is another one of Tim Borski's favorite flies for stalking tailing bonefish.

Hook: Regular saltwater hook, sizes 2 to 1/0.
Thread: Tan flat-waxed nylon.
Tail: Olive marabou, pearl Krystal Flash, and two furnace saddle hackles.
Body: Spun deer hair, clipped very short to the hook shank (do not clip the hair covering the hook point).
Hackle: One grizzly saddle hackle Palmer wrapped over the body.
Eyes: Medium lead dumbbell eyes.

 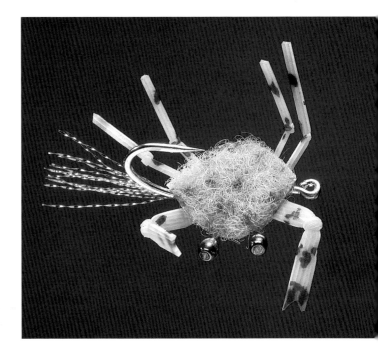

Feather Crab
tied by Capt. Lenny Moffo
Big Pine Key, Florida

Capt. Moffo ties a series of Feather Crabs that are perfect for catching bonefish and permit.

Hook: Regular saltwater hook, size 1/0.
Thread: Brown 6/0.
Tail: Brown Krystal Flash.
Body: Olive felt pad epoxied to the hook shank.
Legs & claws: Golden brown grizzly hackles attached to the bottom of the body with hot glue. The felt body is covering a set of small lead dumbbell eyes.
Eyes: Pieces of 50-pound-test monofilament with beads epoxied to the ends. The eyes are glued to the bottom of the body. After the legs, claws, and eyes are glued in place, cover the bottom of the fly with epoxy and paint white.

Rubber-Legged Feather Crab
tied by Capt. Lenny Moffo
Big Pine Key, Florida

This version of Capt. Moffo's Feather Crab features legs and claws made from rubber bands.

Hook: Regular saltwater hook, size 1/0.
Thread: Tan 6/0.
Tail: Pearl Krystal Flash.
Body: Tan felt pad epoxied to the hook shank and colored with a brown permanent marker.
Legs & claws: Rubber bands colored with permanent markers.
Eyes: Pieces of 50-pound-test monofilament with beads epoxied to the ends. The eyes are glued to the bottom of the body. After the legs, claws, and eyes are glued in place, cover the bottom of the fly with epoxy and paint white.

Shrimp Thing
tied by Capt. Lenny Moffo
Big Pine Key, Florida

*This is another Capt. Moffo original pattern.
He uses this fly to catch redfish and bones'.*

Hook: Regular saltwater hook, sizes 6 to 1.
Thread: Brown 6/0.
Antennae: A small tuft of tan Poly Bear, two strands
of pumpkinseed Sili Legs, and two golden brown
grizzly hackles.
Eyes: Two medium glass eyes.
Body: Pearl Mylar tinsel.
Legs: Two tan hackles Palmer-wrapped up the
hook shank.
Weed guard: 10-pound-test monofilament.

Bone Bug
tied by Capt. Lenny Moffo
Big Pine Key, Florida

*This pattern could just as easily have appeared in
the chapter on tying basic flies; it's a very simple pattern
you'll quickly master. According to Capt. Moffo, "I fish
this fly on flats where I see bonefish as well as permit.
I tie it in a variety of color combinations."*

Hook: Regular saltwater hook, sizes 6 to 1.
Thread: Clear monofilament.
Tail: Pearl Krystal Flash.
Eyes: Small silver bead-chain.
Legs: Orange rubber legs.
Body: Chartreuse chenille.
Wing: Deer or elk hair.

Kwan Fly
tied by Patrick Dorsy
Coral Gables, Florida

The Kwan Fly has been a really hot Keys pattern in recent years. Several guides recommend the Kwan Fly to their clients, and Dorsy reports that the pattern has taken a couple of dozen bonefish weighing over 12 pounds. Those are big bonefish!

Hook: Tiemco TMC800S, size 2.
Thread: Brown Gudebrod size G.
Eyes: Medium lead dumbbell eyes.
Tail: Tan Fly Fur. A brown permanent marker is used to make brown vertical bars. A loop of 30-pound-test monofilament prevents the tail from fouling around the hook.
Body: A small orange pom-pom is tied to the end of the hook shank, followed by pieces of tan and brown rug yarn. Comb out the yarn and clip the body to shape.
Weed guard: 15-pound-test monofilament.

Sam's Toad
tied by Patrick Dorsy
Coral Gables, Florida

Sam's Toad, named for Dorsy's good friend, Sam Bailey, has taken its share of big Islamorada bonefish.

Hook: Tiemco TMC800S, size 2
Thread: Chartreuse Gudebrod size G.
Tail: A tan rabbit strip.
Body: Beige rug yarn clipped to shape and colored with olive and golden-orange permanent markers.
Eyes: Small lead dumbbell eyes.
Weed guard: 15-pound-test monofilament.

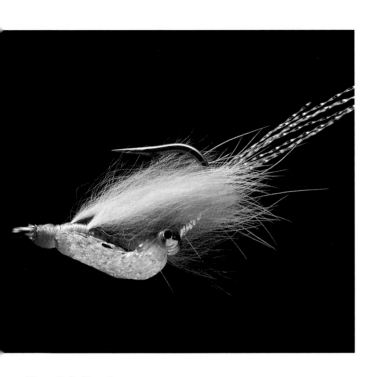

Bonefish Snack
tied by Carter Andrews
Crooked Island, Bahamas

This simple shrimp pattern is used in the Bahamas, but it is worth trying wherever you encounter tailing bonefish.

Hook: Regular saltwater hook, size 6.
Thread: Pink 6/0.
Eyes: Small silver bead-chain.
Antennae: Strands of pearl Krystal Flash. Note that a tag of pearl Krystal Flash is wrapped down into the bend of the hook.
Body: Pink tying thread.
Wing: Tufts of tan rabbit fur.
Shell: A strip of pearl Mylar braid tied in at the end of the hook shank, folded over the top of the hook, tied off, clipped, and coated with epoxy.

chapter 7

MORE THAN ONE WAY TO CATCH A FLY

Epoxy and silicone have had a tremendous impact on fly tying. Throughout this book we have seen flies where the use of epoxy, and to a lesser extent silicone, have been used to construct flies. In this chapter we'll examine these materials in more detail. And for our tying demonstration, we'll look at one of the most important styles of patterns in saltwater, the Surf Candy.

It's impossible to discuss tying saltwater epoxy flies without mentioning New Jersey's Bob Popovics. With the way he uses materials, especially epoxy and silicone, you might say that his patterns are revolutionary. When his flies started receiving publicity, fly-tying purists were aghast at his generous use of high-tech glues. These guys seemed to think that everything had to be lashed to hooks with thread, and that Bob's methods weren't true fly tying. A few even suggested that Bob's techniques were a type of cheating, and discussions raged about whether his patterns should be considered real flies at all.

I'll let you decide whether Bob Popovics's patterns are "real" flies, and whether or not you'd like to "tie" them. Personally, I like his flies; they're realistic and durable, and they catch fish. His patterns are also fun to make.

For a fuller explanation of Bob's tying methods and patterns, I suggest you read the book *Pop Fleyes*, by Ed Jaworowski and Bob Popovics. This is a complete treatise on the entire Popovics family of flies. For our tying exercise, I'm going to demonstrate how to tie a generic Surf Candy, the term Bob uses to refer to his family of epoxy-headed baitfish flies. Later, you can select the colors of materials and tie the flies in sizes to match your local baitfish.

In the selection of guides's flies at the end of this chapter, you'll find a range of patterns using epoxy and silicone as major fly-tying components. Some of these flies are direct descendants of Bob's patterns, and they will give you more ideas about how to create these neat patterns.

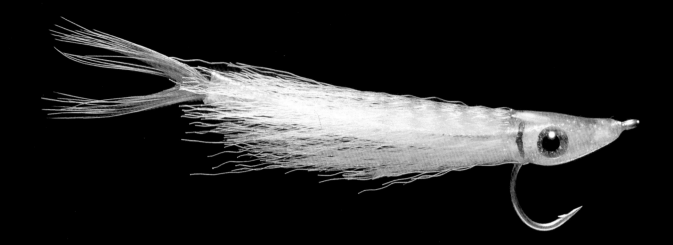

Surf Candy

Surf Candy—what a neat name for a fly. There are Surf Candies that represent a wide variety of important baitfish—anchovies, mullet, menhaden, and spearing are just a few examples. These are all major prey species for gamefish, and the Surf Candy style of tying can be used to create flies that match all of them.

A Surf Candy has two main features. The first is a body made from some long-fibered material. Bucktail may be used to tie small Surf Candies, but the bodies of most Surf Candies are crafted from some sort of synthetic hair—FisHair and Ultra Hair are two common examples.

An epoxy head is the second key feature of a Surf Candy. Clear five-minute epoxy is commonly used to make the heads on Surf Candies, but this material hardens quickly so you must work fast. It's almost impossible to tie a batch of Surf Candies using five-minute epoxy, and novice tiers might be frustrated with the lack of working time. If you're new to tying Surf Candies and plan to work slowly, or if you'd like to tie several Surf Candies at a time, select the widely available 2-Ton Epoxy. This material has about a thirty minute working time.

I'm going to tie a fairly generic Surf Candy using "fishy" colored materials without tying a pattern that matches a specific species of baitfish. But this

isn't an idle tying exercise. I use this pattern in my local estuaries in the fall with great success. At that time of the year, migrating striped bass pass by on their trek south. There are no large runs of baitfish, but I use this fly to catch my share of fish. The point in this exercise is to learn how to tie a Surf Candy; later you can select materials in the colors that match your local baitfish. The Surf Candy is more a style of tying than a specific pattern, and you can adapt the tying methods to create a wide variety of baitfish imitations.

Surf Candy

Hook: Regular saltwater hook, sizes 6 to 1/0.

Thread: Fine clear monofilament thread.

Tail: Saddle hackle clipped to form a chevron and tied to a piece of 20-pound-test monofilament.

Underbody: Narrow silver or pearl Mylar tubing.

Body: FisHair, Ultra Hair or a similar material in your choice of colors.

Eyes: Medium silver adhesive eyes.

Gills: Red permanent marker.

Head: Epoxy.

Step 1
Start the Surf Candy by making the tail and underbody. Begin by clipping a saddle hackle into the shape of a chevron. Tie the feather to the end of a 5-inch-long piece of 20-pound-test monofilament.

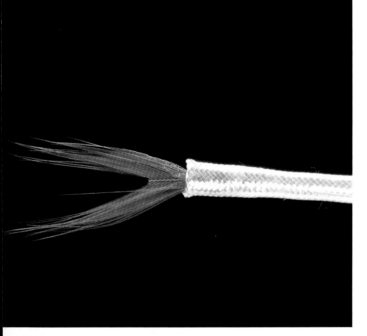

Step 2
Remove the cotton core from a piece of Mylar tubing. Slip the tubing onto the monofilament. Tie off the end of the tubing at the base of the feather tail. Tie off and clip the thread, and apply a drop of cement to the thread knot. Push a small amount of tubing back on itself (as shown in the photo) to create a neat underbody.

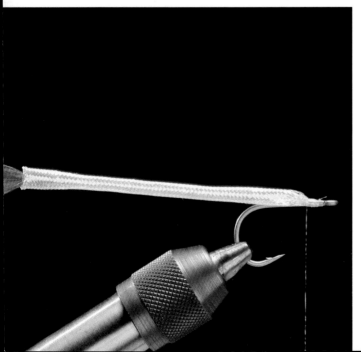

Step 3
Hold the tubing and monofilament over the hook to determine the correct length for the underbody, and clip the excess tubing and mono. Tie the tubing to the top of the hook.

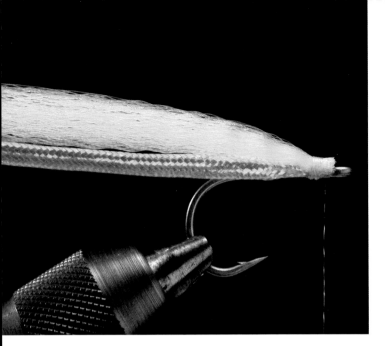

Step 4

Tie a bunch of synthetic hair material (I'm using yellow Ultra Hair) to the top of the underbody.

Step 5

Using your thumb and forefinger, spread the synthetic hair down the sides of the underbody. Note that there is a little more hair under than on top of the underbody.

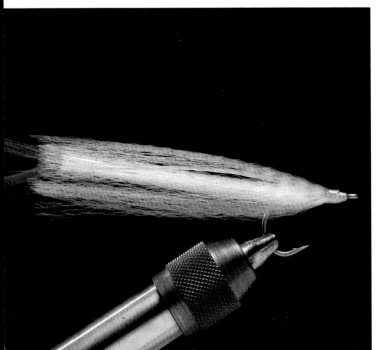

Step 6

Tie another bunch of synthetic hair to form the back of the fly (I'm using green Ultra Hair). All of the hair is extending to the base of the feather tail. I'll clip the hair to final length as the last step in completing the Surf Candy.

Step 7

Apply a coat of epoxy on the head area of the fly. Use a bodkin needle to force some of the epoxy between the hairs and into the center of the head. Work quickly before the epoxy thickens. Allow the epoxy to fully cure before proceeding. Place an adhesive eye on each side of the head. The gills are made with a red permanent marker.

Step 8

Apply a second coat of epoxy. Be sure that the first coat has fully cured before applying the second coat or the head might look dull. I allow the first application to cure for twenty-four hours before finishing the fly.

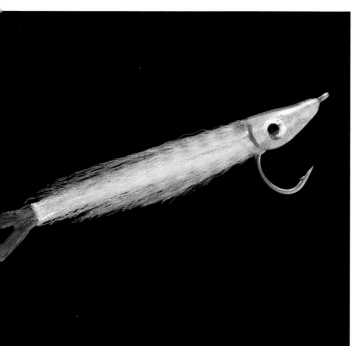

Step 9

The final step is to clip the synthetic hair around the base of the tail and give the body of the fly a tapered appearance like a real baitfish. The realistic silhouette of the Surf Candy is one of the most important attributes of this pattern.

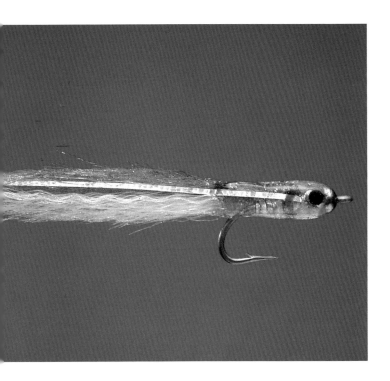

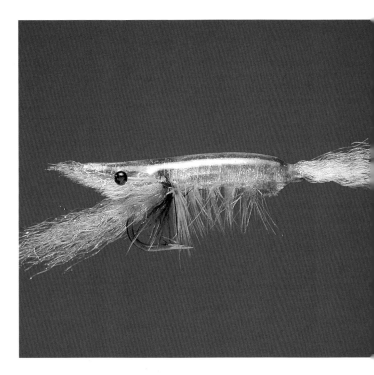

Albie Candy
tied by Peter Vincelette
Lakewood, New Jersey

This Bob Popovics style pattern is a good choice for when the false albicore and bonito are running. In addition to brown and white, Peter ties this fly in a variety of colors including olive, chartreuse, gray, green, and black.

Hook: Regular saltwater hook, sizes 6 and 4.
Thread: Clear monofilament.
Weight: Small tungsten bead.
Underbody: Silver holographic tinsel wrapped on the hook shank.
Body: Brown and white Unique Hair, and a strip of silver holographic tinsel tied on each side for the lateral lines. Coat the head of the fly with five-minute epoxy.
Eyes: Small silver adhesive eyes.
Gills: Red permanent marker.

Super Shrimp
tied by Peter Vincelette
Lakewood, New Jersey

The Super Shrimp is at home on the Northeast coast or the Florida flats—wherever gamefish feed on shrimp. Tie this pattern in colors to match the local shrimp.

Hook: Regular saltwater hook, sizes 4 and 2.
Thread: Clear monofilament.
Antennae: Tan Super Hair.
Eyes: Melted 30-pound-test monofilament.
Body: Tan Super Hair. Allow the Super Hair to extend out over the hook eye to form the tail of the shrimp, and out over the hook bend to form the head.
Legs: Ginger hackle Palmer-wrapped over the body. Clip the hackle fibers from the top of the fly.
Shell back: Five-minute epoxy.

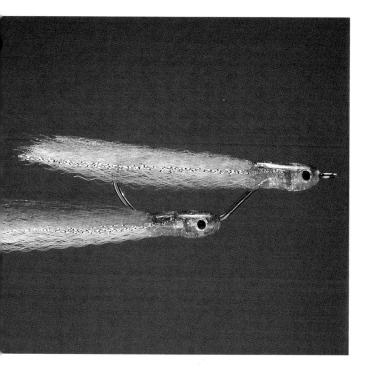

Schoolie
tied by Peter Vincelette
Lakewood, New Jersey

Here's another Bob Popovics pattern. Try this duo when you're confident that you can make both flies look pretty much the same. Peter Vincelette did an excellent job on this unique pattern.

Hook: Keel fly hook (such as the Mustad 79666S), size 2/0.
Thread: White, size A.
Underbodies: Silver holographic tinsel.
Bodies: White and olive Super Hair with strands of silver Krystal Flash. Coat the head of the flies with five-minute epoxy.
Eyes: Small silver adhesive eyes.
Gills: Red permanent marker.

Ever-Ready
tied by Capt. Doug Jowett
Brunswick, Maine

The Ever-Ready is a bright, translucent fly that does a good job at imitating a variety of small minnow-shaped baitfish.

Hook: Regular saltwater hook, size 2.
Thread: Clear monofilament.
Weight: Small tungsten cone.
Body: Pearl Krystal Flash and Flashabou. Coat the front section of the body and the tungsten cone with five-minute epoxy.
Eyes: Small yellow adhesive eyes.
Gills: Red permanent marker.

Reggie's Blue Claw Crab
tied by Richard "Reggie" Regensburg
Ocean View, New Jersey

Yes, crabs do swim. And yes, big fish feed on crabs. "Reggie" Regensburg has used his Blue Claw Crab to catch stripped bass and weakfish, and he knows other anglers who have used this inventive fly to catch Florida permit.

Hook: Mustad 34011, size 1/0.
Thread: Clear monofilament.
Body: Upholstery foam clipped to shape, colored with permanent markers and coated with clear silicone.
Legs & Claws: White or cream hackles colored with permanent markers.

MOG Glass Minnow
tied by Capt. Ron Kowalyk
Ft. Myers, Florida

The Mother of Glue Glass Minnow is an all-around utility fly. Capt. Kowalyk uses this pattern to catch snook, redfish, sea trout, ladyfish, and jacks. In the Northeast it would easily catch strippers and bluefish. It is an unusual pattern that fits neatly into this chapter about flies made from epoxy and silicone—and now hot glue.

Hook: Mustad 3407, sizes 2 to 1/0.
Thread: White flat-waxed nylon.
Eyes: Large black plastic bead-chain.
Tail: White bucktail and pearl Krystal Flash. Coat the head of the fly between the bead-chain eyes with hot glue.

Moff's Minnow
tied by Capt. Lenny Moffo
Big Pine Key, Florida

Hook: Mustad 34011, sizes 2 to 3/0.
Thread: Chartreuse Monocord.
Tail: Chartreuse marabou with strands of gold Flashabou.
Body: Pearl Mylar tubing tied on the hook shank and pressed flat. Dip the head of the fly in red dye. Add a black stripe down the back of the fly using a permanent marker. Coat the body with five-minute epoxy.
Eyes: Medium red adhesive eyes.

Lenny's Redfish Wobble Fly
tied by Capt. Lenny Moffo
Big Pine Key, Florida

The Wobble Fly is a neat concept that can be used to craft flies that catch many species of fish. The style of body gives the fly a unique quaking action when stripped through the water. Capt. Moffo uses this version for redfish, but it undoubtedly has wider applications.

Hook: Bend-Back hook, sizes 1 to 2/0.
Thread: Brown Monocord.
Body: Gold Mylar tubing, tied on the hook shank, flattened, and coated with five-minute epoxy.
Eyes: Small orange adhesive eyes.
Wing: Brown calf tail hair and two golden-brown grizzly hackles.

Buckshot Bonefish
tied by Capt. Lenny Moffo
Big Pine Key, Florida

Hook: Regular saltwater hook, sizes 6 to 2.
Thread: Brown Monocord.
Tail: A small tuft of tan Poly Bear and two pumpkin-seed Sili Legs.
Body: Gold Mylar tubing, tied to the hook and pressed flat. Coat the tubing with five-minute epoxy.
Eyes: No. 6 birdshot (place a piece of birdshot on each side of the body as the epoxy hardens).
Wing: Tan Poly Bear (use a brown permanent marker to add brown vertical markings).

Veil Fly
tied by Bob Lindquist
East Patchoque, New York

The Veil Fly, which can be tied from small to the largest sizes—up to 9/0—requires only a couple of ingredients. It is similar to the popular freshwater Thunder Creek Minnow in which the body materials are tied pointing forward over the hook eye and then folded back, and the head is coated with head cement, epoxy, or some other material. Tier Bob Lindquist recommends coating the head of the Veil Fly with Softex.

Hook: Gamakatsu SC15, size 2.
Thread: White Monocord, size 3/0.
Body: White EP Fibers mixed with pearl-blue Angel Hair on the bottom, and strands of pearl Glimmer. Tie the materials on pointing forward over the hook eye, fold back, and apply a thin coat of Softex on the head.
Eyes: Extra-small white adhesive eyes.

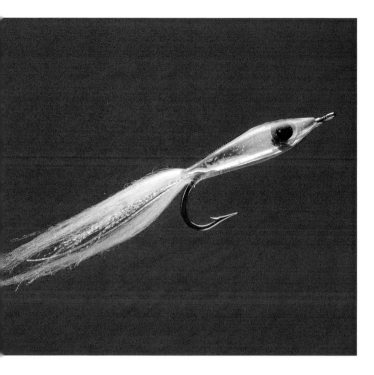

The Holo Minnow
tied by Capt. Russ Shirley
St. Petersburg, Florida

Hook: Long-shank saltwater hook, size 2.
Thread: Fine clear monofilament thread.
Weight: Narrow lead wire wrapped on the hook shank.
Tail: A soft white hair material such as EP Fibers and strands of pearl Krystal Flash.
Body: A piece of silver holographic tape, clipped to shape and placed on each side of the hook shank. Coat the top, bottom and sides of the body with five-minute epoxy.
Gills: Red permanent marker.
Eyes: Medium silver adhesive eyes.

Butt Ugly
tied by Capt. Russ Shirley
St. Petersburg, Florida

Hook: Long-shank saltwater hook, size 2.
Thread: Fine clear monofilament thread.
Weight: Narrow lead wire wrapped on the hook shank.
Tail: A soft white hair material such as EP Fibers and strands of pearl Krystal Flash.
Body: Pearl EZ Body tubing. Tie the tubing to the hook, and color the back of the fly with a green permanent marker and the belly with a red permanent marker. Coat the tubing with five-minute epoxy.
Eyes: Medium white doll eyes.

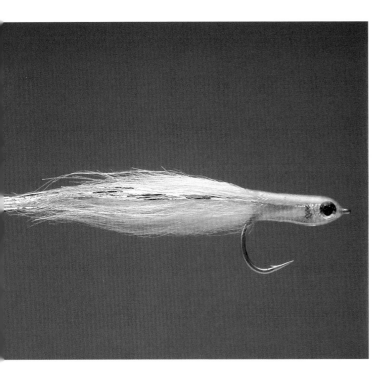

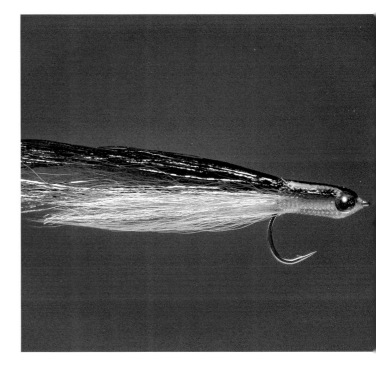

Finesse Fly Glass Minnow
tied by Capt. Gary Dubiel
Oriental, North Carolina

This is another of Capt. Dubiel's patterns that catches a wide variety of fish: false albacore, Spanish mackerel, bonito, and bluefish.

Hook: Regular saltwater hook, sizes 4 to 1.
Thread: Fine clear monofilament thread.
Tail: White craft fur, tan craft fur and silver Krienik's Flash-n-Tube.
Head: Medium clear EZ Body tubing coated with five-minute epoxy.
Eyes: Small silver adhesive eyes.

Finesse Fly Silverside
tied by Capt. Gary Dubiel
Oriental, North Carolina

The Finesse Fly Silverside is an excellent utility fly. According to Capt. Dubiel, it has been used to catch eighteen species of fish, including sea trout, red drum, flounder, striped bass, bluefish, weakfish, and Spanish mackerel. It is a good fly to try throughout the year.

Hook: Regular saltwater hook, size 1/0.
Thread: Fine clear monofilament thread.
Tail: White bucktail, green bucktail, pearl Bill's Bodi Braid picked out, silver Krienik's Flash-n-Tube and damselfly-green Krienik's Flash-n-Tube.
Body: Pearl "Minnow Maker" EZ Body tubing coated with five-minute epoxy.
Eyes: Medium silver dome eyes.

appendix Select Bibliography

Fly fishing and tying have a very rich literary tradition. The vast majority of this literature describes fishing and dressing flies to catch trout; the number of books about saltwater angling lags far behind. In recent years, along with the growing interest in tossing flies to big saltwater gamefish, there has been a surge in books about saltwater fly fishing. Below are some of my favorites; I think you will learn a lot by adding one or more of these great books to your reading list. Let me point out that this is not an exhaustive list of all saltwater fly-fishing books—far from it—but this selection contains some of the best.

Pop Fleyes, by Ed Jaworowski and Bob Popovics, Stackpole Books, 2001.

Fly-Fishing the Saltwater Shoreline, by Ed Mitchell, Stackpole Books, 2001.

Bonefish Fly Patterns, by Dick Brown, Lyons & Burford, 1996.

Innovative Saltwater Flies, by Bob Veverka, Stackpole Books, 1999.

Inshore Fly Fishing, by Lou Tabory, Lyons & Burford, 1992.

A Fly-Fisher's Guide to Saltwater Naturals and Their Imitation, by George V. Roberts, Jr., Ragged Mountain Press, 1994.

Saltwater Fly Patterns, by Lefty Kreh, Lyons & Burford, 1995.

The Fisherman's Ocean: How Marine Science Can Help You Catch More Fish, by Dr. David A. Ross, Stackpole Books, 2000.

There are also several periodicals that contain a wealth of information for saltwater fly anglers. Once again, the following is just a partial list of what's available.

Fly Tyer
American Angler
Saltwater Fly Fishing
Fly Fishing Salt Waters
Florida Sportsman
Fly Fisherman

appendix

All of the following guides and tiers have flies featured in this book or helped me in other important ways in preparing this book. These folks know how to craft flies that fool fish. Many thanks to all of them for their help.

Carter Andrews
Pittstown Point Landings
Crooked Island, Bahamas
242-344-2507

Tim Borski
P.O. Box 122
Islamorada, FL 33036
305-852-9886
jzimakeys@aol.com

Capt. Christopher Dean
5775 S.W. 54 Terrace
Miami, FL 33155
305-666-0908

Patrick Dorsy
6580 Santona Street, #12
Coral Gables, FL 33146
305-519-6164
Patdorsy1@aol.com

Brian Dowd
Tidewater Flies
33 Shady Lane
Hardyston, NJ 07419
973-827-2210
twf@tidewaterflies.com

Capt. Gary Dubiel
Spec Fever
P.O. Box 1029
9506 Connie Cove
Oriental, NC 28571
252-249-1520
captgary@specfever.com

Captain James Ellis
4178 Curch Street
West Barnstable,
   MA 02668
508-362-9108
jellis@gis.net

Pat Ford
9510 S.W. 136 St.
Miami, FL 33176
305-670-2000
TPFORDJR@aol.com

Capt. Gary Graham
Baja On the Fly
P.O. Box 300189
Escondido, CA 92030
800-919-2252
bajafly@usa.net

Capt. John Haag
17 Book Nursery Drive
Brookhaven, NY 11719

Capt. Kris Jop
Come Fly With Me
   Fishing Charters
547 Front Street
Marion, MA 02738
877-266-3359
seafly@four.net

Capt. Doug Jowett
61 Four Wheel Drive
Brunswick, ME 04011
207-725-4573

Capt. Larry Kennedy
3405 Frederica Road
St. Simons Island
   GA 31522
912-638-5454
lkennedy@gate.net

Capt. Ron Kowalyk
19049 Murcott Drive
   West
Ft. Myers, FL 33912
941-267-9312
captronkowalyk
   @webtv. net

Capt. Richard Kress
Osprey Ltd.
556 Alden Drive
Rahway, NJ 07065
732-388-3086
ospreyltd@msn.com

Justin Krul
English Angling Trappings
P.O. Box 8885
New Fairfield, CT 06812
203-746-4121
alcoif@aol.com

Capt. Ken Kuhner
Cold Spring Outfitters
37 Main Street
Cold Spring Harbor,
   NY 11724
631-6738937
captken@villagenet.com

Bob Lindquist
7 Thompson Street
East Patchoque, NY
11772

Capt. Dan Malzone
Saltwater Outfitters, Inc.
4709 Cherokee Road
Tampa, FL 33629
813-831-4052
capt.dan.malzone
   @worldnet.att.net

Tom McQuade
P.O. Box 161
St. John, U.S. Virgin
   Islands
340-693-9446
tom.mcquade@att.net

Capt. Lenny Moffo
3978 Diane Road
Big Pine Key, FL 33043
305-872-4683
captlen@earthlink.net

Richard Murphy
25 Warren Street
Georgetown, MA 01833
978-352-7893

Frank S. Oblak
17865 S.W. 174 St.
Miami, FL 33187
305-253-4018

appendix

Jeffrey Pierce
8 Church Street
Scottsville, NY 14546
315-253-2793
jeff@mustad-usa.com

Enrico Puglisi
55 West Hills Road
Huntingdon Station, NY
  11746
631-427-2387
epflies@earthlink.net

Richard "Reggie"
  Regensburg
1542 S. Shore Road
Ocean View, NJ 08230
609-390-9199
grubs@bellatlantic.net

Capt. Len Roberts
On the Flie
P.O. Box 1479
Islamorada, FL 33036
305-664-5420
ontheflie@aol.com

Capt. Bob Robl
Fly A-Salt
3 Kilmer Avenue
Dix Hills, NJ 11746
631-243-4282
RTROBL@cs.com

Capt. Bob Rodgers
P.O. Box 1510
Tavernier, FL 33070
305-853-0933
brodgers@ddtcom.com

Capt. Russ Shirley
Salty Fly Charters
7111 3rd Ave. S.
St. Petersburg, FL 33707
727-343-1957
russ@captruss.com

Capt. Dexter Simmons
17240 Oleander Lane
Sugarloaf Shores,
  FL 33042
305-745-3304
captdexter@prodigy.net

Capt. Roy String
Fish'n Addiction Charters
3553 Beneva Lane
Sarasota, FL 34231
941-379-5083
roystring@aol.com

Capt. Ed Wasicki
Skinnywater
  Flyfishing Co.
3818 Sunbeam Court
Merritt Island, FL 32953
407-449-0300

Capt. Jim White
White Ghost
43 York Drive
Coventry, RI 02816
401-828-9465
whiteghos1@aol.com

index

A

Abel Vise, 3, 4
Albie Candy, 138
Alewives, Glimmer Herring for, 57
Amberjack, JP's Flying Fish for, 61
American Eel, RM, 104
Andrews, Carter, 147
  Bonefish Snack, 131
  Permit Snack, 124
  Tuna Snack, 61
Angel Hair Zonker, 47
Apte, Stu
  Tarpon Fly, 63, 64–66
  Tarpon Fly II, 67–71
Apte II, 67–71
Aquatic grass. *See* Flats flies
Art's Shrimp, 80–86

B

Baby Bunker, 46
Baitfish flies. *See* Epoxy flies;
  Small baitfish flies
Baja Deepdiver, 47
Banded Shrimp, 100
Barracuda, flies for
  'Cuda Fly, 17–20
  'Cuda Killer, 30
  Everything Fly, 125
  JP's Flying Fish, 61
  Pink Imitator Shrimp, 121
  Utility Minnow, 55
  the Whistler, 12–16
Basic flies, 11–31
  Bend-Back, 21–25
  C. H. Woolly Bugger
    Express, 30
  Chartreuse & White
    Seducer, 26
  'Cuda Fly, 17–20
  'Cuda Killer, 30
  Deceiver, 27
  Frank's Roosterfish Fly, 31
  Ice Cream Cone, 27
  Llamaceiver, 28
  the Nothin' Honey, 29
  Red & White Bend-Back, 26
  See-Through Deceiver, 28
  Stringbean, 29
  the Whistler, 12–16

Bass Magic, 48
Bay Anchovies, 34–38
  by Ken Kuhner, 49
  by Rich Murphy, 34, 50
Bend-Backs, 21–25
  Red & White, 26
Big-Bellied Silverside, 56
Black Death, 72
  Malzone's, 76
Black drum, MOG Crab for, 125
Black Fly, 77
Blenny, Lenny's, 126
Blondie, Malzone's, 75
Bluefish, flies for
  Deceiver, 27
  Epoxy Sand Eel, 101
  Finesse Fly Glass Minnow, 144
  Finesse Fly Silverside, 144
  Five-Feather Herring, 52
  MOG Glass Minnow, 140
  RM American Eel, 104
  RM Flatside 2, 51
  squid and eel for, 79
  Utility Minnow, 55
  the Whistler, 12–16
Bob's Bread and Butter, 73
Bob's Tarpon Crab, 73
Bodkins, 5
Bone Bug, 129
Bonefish, flies for
  Banded Shrimp, 100
  Bend-Backs, 21–25, 26
  Bone Bug, 129
  Bonefish Snack, 131
  Bristle Worm, 127
  Buckshot Bonefish, 142
  Chernobyl Crab, 127
  Everything Fly, 125
  Feather Crab, 128
  Fuzzy Shrimp, 101
  Kwan Fly, 130
  Lenny's Blenny, 126
  Len's False Pichard, 126
  Mega Shrimp 2, 106
  the Other Crab, 120
  Pink Imitator Shrimp, 121
  Rootbeer Sugarloaf
    Special, 118
  Sam's Toad, 130
  Shrimp Thing, 129
  Tan E-Z Crab, 121
  the Thing, 122

Bonefish Snack, 131
Bonito, flies for
  Albie Candy, 138
  Bay Anchovy, 34–38, 49
  Finesse Fly Glass Minnow, 144
  Kris's Bonito Special, 53
  RM Flatside 2, 51
Boomer, 51
Borski, Tim, 109, 119, 147
  Bristle Worm, 127
  Chernobyl Crab, 127
  Green Zima, 74
Bread and Butter, Bob's, 73
Bristle Worm, 127
Bubble Shrimp, Reggie's, 106
Buckshot Bonefish, 142
Bugger Shrimp, 102
Butt Ugly, 143

C

C. H. Woolly Bugger
  Express, 30
Chartreuse & White
  Seducer, 26
Chernobyl Crab, 127
Cinnamon Cactus Chenille
  Shrimp, 105
Circle hooks, 6–7, 45, 101
Cobia, flies for
  Feather Pup, 54
  Lenny's Tarpon Shrimp, 107
  Len's False Pichard, 126
Cochran, Vaughn, 77
Crabs (crab flies)
  Bob's Tarpon Crab, 73
  Chernobyl Crab, 127
  Critter Crabs, 109, 110–114, 119
  Dean Permit Crab, 119
  Feather Crab, 128
  MOG Crab, 125
  the Other Crab, 120
  Reggie's Blue Claw Crab, 140
  Rockin' Crabs, 109, 115–117, 124
  Rubber-Legged Feather
    Crab, 128
  Tan E-Z Crab, 121

Critter Crabs, 109, 110–114, 119
'Cuda Fly, 17–20
'Cuda Killer, 30

D

Dean, Christopher, 147
  Chartreuse & White
    Seducer, 26
  Critter Crabs, 109, 110–114, 119
  Dean Permit Crab, 119
  Emery Epoxy Fly, 120
  Red & White Bend-Back, 26
Dean Permit Crab, 119
Deceivers, 27, 64
  Llamaceiver, 28
  See-Through, 28
DJ Hi-Ti, 53
Dolphin, JP's Flying Fish for, 61
Dorado, See-Through
  Deceiver for, 28
Dorsy, Patrick, 147
  Kwan Fly, 130
  Sam's Toad, 130
Dowd, Brian, 147
Dubbing loops (brushes), 102
Dubiel, Gary, 145
  Finesse Fly Glass Minnow, 144
  Finesse Fly Silverside, 144
  Lil' Hadden, 45
Dyna-King Vise, 3, 4

E

Eel (eel flies), 79
  Epoxy Sand Eel, 101
  EZ Eel, 95–99
  RM American Eel, 104
  Sand Eel, 102
Ellis, James, 147
  Angel Hair Zonker, 47
  Baby Bunker, 46
  Deceiver, 27
  Epoxy Sand Eel, 101
  Gotcha' Clouser, 45
  Sand Eel, 102
  Silverside, 46

index

Emery Epoxy Fly, 120
Epoxy (and silicone) flies,
    133–144
    Albie Candy, 138
    Bay Anchovy, 34–38
    Buckshot Bonefish, 142
    Butt Ugly, 143
    Emery Epoxy Fly, 120
    Epoxy Sand Eel, 101
    Ever-Ready, 139
    Finesse Fly Glass Minnow,
        144
    Finesse Fly Silverside, 144
    Holo Minnow, 143
    Lenny's Redfish Wobble
        Fly, 141
    Moff's Minnow, 141
    MOG Glass Minnow, 140
    Reggie's Blue Claw Crab,
        140
    Schoolie, 139
    Super Shrimp, 138
    Surf Candy, 133, 134–137
    Veil Fly, 142
Ever-Ready, 139
Everything Fly, 125
EZ Eel, 95–99

F

False albacore, flies for
    Albie Candy, 138
    Bay Anchovy, 34–38, 49
    Finesse Fly Glass Minnow,
        144
    JP's Flying Fish, 61
    Kris's Bonito Special, 53
    RM Flatside 2, 51
False Pichard, Len's, 126
Feather Crabs, 128
    Rubber-Legged, 128
Feather Pup, 54
Feathers (hackles), 8
Fernandez, Chico
    Bend-Back, 21–25
    on tarpon patterns, 64
Finesse Fly Glass Minnow,
    144
Finesse Fly Silverside, 144
FisHair, 9, 134
Five-Feather Herring, 52
Flash materials, 2, 9
Flashabou, 2, 9

Flats flies, 109–131
    Banded Shrimp, 100
    Bend-Backs, 21–25, 26
    Bone Bug, 129
    Bonefish Snack, 131
    Bristle Worm, 127
    characteristics of, 109
    Chernobyl Crab, 127
    Critter Crabs, 109,
        110–114, 119
    Dean Permit Crab, 119
    Emery Epoxy Fly, 120
    Everything Fly, 125
    Feather Crab, 128
    Kwan Fly, 130
    Lenny's Blenny, 126
    Len's False Pichard, 126
    MOG Crab, 125
    Olive Sugarloaf Special,
        118
    the Other Crab, 120
    the Other Thing (Dark
        Tan), 123
    the Other Thing (Light
        Tan), 123
    Pearl Imitator Shrimp, 122
    Permit Snack, 124
    Pink Imitator Shrimp, 121
    Rockin' Crabs, 109,
        115–117, 124
    Rootbeer Sugarloaf
        Special, 118
    Rubber-Legged Feather
        Crab, 128
    Sam's Toad, 130
    Shrimp Thing, 129
    Tan E-Z Crab, 121
    the Thing, 122
Flounder, flies for
    Finesse Fly Silverside, 144
    Lil' Hadden, 45
Fluke, Green Ghost for, 52
Flying Fish, JP's, 61
Ford, Pat, 145
    Mega Shrimp, 105
    Mega Shrimp 2, 106
Frank's Roosterfish Fly, 31
Fuzzy Shrimp, 101

G

Glimmer Bunker, 56
Glimmer Herring, 57

Glimmer Pinfish, 57
Gotcha' Clouser, 45
Graham, Gary, 145
    Baja Deepdiver, 47
    See-Through Deceiver, 28
Green Ghost, 52
Green Hornet, 72
Green Zima, 74

H

Haag, John, 147
    Big-Bellied Silverside, 56
    Glimmer Bunker, 56
    Glimmer Herring, 57
    Glimmer Pinfish, 57
    No-Bay-Vy, 58
    Rainfish, 58
    Spring Lance, 59
    Woolly Mullet, 59
    Woolly Mummichog, 60
Hackles, 8
Herring flies, 51, 52, 57
Hickory shad, Ice Cream
    Cone for, 27
Holo Minnow, 143
Hooks, 6–7
    designed for Bend-Backs,
        21
    vise buying tips and, 3

I

Ice Cream Cone, 27

J

Jacks, flies for
    C. H. Woolly Bugger
        Express, 30
    MOG Glass Minnow, 140
    RM Flatside 2, 51
    See-Through Deceiver, 28
    Utility Minnow, 55
Jail Bait, 55
Jop, Kris, 145
    Kris's Bonito Special, 53
Jowett, Doug, 145
    DJ Hi-Ti, 53
    Ever-Ready, 139
    Five-Feather Herring, 52
JP's Flying Fish, 61

JP's Mini Mack, 60
Jumpin' Shrimp, 107

K

Kennedy, Larry, 145
    C. H. Woolly Bugger
        Express, 30
Kowalyk, Ron, 147
    Cinnamon Cactus
        Chenille Shrimp, 105
    MOG Crab, 125
    MOG Glass Minnow,
        140
    the Nothin' Honey, 29
    Soda Straw Shrimp, 104
Kress, Richard, 147
Kris's Bonito Special, 53
Krul, Justin, 147
    Ice Cream Cone, 27
Kuhner, Ken, 147
    Bay Anchovy, 49
    Spearing, 49
Kwan Fly, 130

L

Ladyfish, C. H. Woolly
    Bugger Express for, 30
Lefty's Deceiver. See
    Deceivers
Lenny's Blenny, 126
Lenny's Redfish Wobble Fly,
    141
Lenny's Tarpon Shrimp, 107
Len's False Pichard, 126
Len's Tarpon Ocean Runner,
    75
Lil' Hadden, 45
Lindquist, Bob, 147
    Bugger Shrimp, 102
    Llamaceiver, 28
    Silverside Muddler, 48
    Veil Fly, 142
Llamaceiver, 28

M

McQuade, Tom, 147
    Banded Shrimp, 100
    Fuzzy Shrimp, 101
    the Other Crab, 120

the Other Thing (Dark Tan), 123
the Other Thing (Light Tan), 123
Pearl Imitator Shrimp, 122
Pink Imitator Shrimp, 121
Tan E-Z Crab, 121
the Thing, 122
Trashline Squid, 100
Malzone, Dan, 145
Black Death, 76
Blondie, 75
Purple Demon, 76
Materials, 2, 6–9. *See also specific materials*
buying tips, 2
synthetic, 2, 8–9
Mega Shrimp, 105
Mega Shrimp 2, 106
Menhadens, 39
Mini Mack, JP's, 60
Minnows (minnow flies)
Finesse Fly Glass Minnow, 144
Holo Minnow, 143
Moff's Minnow, 141
MOG Glass Minnow, 140
Utility Minnow, 55
Moffo, Lenny, 147
Black Fly, 77
Bone Bug, 129
Buckshot Bonefish, 142
'Cuda Killer, 30
Feather Crab, 128
Feather Pup, 54
Jail Bait, 55
Jumpin' Shrimp, 107
Lenny's Redfish Wobble Fly, 141
Lenny's Tarpon Shrimp, 107
Moff's Minnow, 141
Rubber-Legged Feather Crab, 128
Sea Pup, 54
Shrimp Thing, 129
Tarpon Toy, 77
Utility Minnow, 55
MOG Crab, 125
MOG Glass Minnow, 140
Murphy, Richard, 147
Boomer, 51
RM American Eel, 104

RM Bay Anchovy, 34, 50
RM Flatside 2, 51
RM Shortfin Squid, 87–94
RM Soft Short, 103
RM Spitfire, 50
RM Sting, 103

N

Needlefish, 17, 63
No-Bay-Vy, 58
Nothin' Honey, the, 29

O

Oblak, Frank, 145
Frank's Roosterfish Fly, 31
Olive Sugarloaf Special, 118
Other Crab, the, 120
Other Thing, the
Dark Tan, 123
Light Tan, 123

P

Peacock bass, Frank's Roosterfish Fly for, 31
Peanut Bunker, Enrico's, 39–44
Pearl Imitator Shrimp, 122
Periodicals, 145
Permit, flies for
Dean Permit Crab, 119
Everything Fly, 125
Feather Crab, 128
Lenny's Blenny, 126
Lenny's Tarpon Shrimp, 107
Mega Shrimp 2, 106
the Other Crab, 120
Permit Snack, 124
Sugarloaf Specials, 118
the Thing, 122
Permit Snack, 124
Pierce, Jeffrey, 148
JP's Flying Fish, 61
JP's Mini Mack, 60
Pinfish, 55
Pink Imitator Shrimp, 121
Pompano, MOG Crab for, 125

Popovics, Bob, 133, 138, 139
Puglisi, Enrico, Peanut Bunker, 39–44
Purple Demon, Malzone's, 76

R

Rainfish, 58
Razor blades, single-edged, 5
Red & White Bend-Back, 26
Red Death, 74
Red drum, Finesse Fly Silverside for, 144
Redfish, flies for, 79
Bend-Back, 21–25, 26
Emery Epoxy Fly, 120
Frank's Roosterfish Fly, 31
Lenny's Redfish Wobble Fly, 141
Len's False Pichard, 126
Lil' Hadden, 45
MOG Crab, 125
MOG Glass Minnow, 140
the Nothin' Honey, 29
Red & White Bend-Back, 26
RM Flatside 2, 51
the Rockin' Crab, 124
Shrimp Thing, 129
Stringbean, 29
Texas coast flats for, 109
Regensburg, Dick "Reggie," 145
Blue Claw Crab, 140
Bubble Shrimp, 106
RM American Eel, 104
RM Bay Anchovy, 34, 50
RM Flatside 2, 51
RM Shortfin Squid, 87–94
RM Soft Short, 103
RM Spitfire, 50
RM Sting, 103
Roberts, Len, 145
Everything Fly, 125
Lenny's Blenny, 126
Len's False Pichard, 126
Len's Tarpon Ocean Runner, 75
Red Death, 74
Robl, Bob, 145
Bass Magic, 48

Rockin' Crabs, 109, 115–117, 124
Rodgers, Bob, 148
Bob's Bread and Butter, 73
Bob's Tarpon Crab, 73
Roosterfish, flies for
Frank's Roosterfish Fly, 31
RM Flatside 2, 51
See-Through Deceiver, 28
Rootbeer Sugarloaf Special, 118
Rubber-Legged Feather Crab, 128
Rug yarn, 110

S

Saddle hackles, 8
Saltwater hooks, 6–7
Sam's Toad, 130
Sand Eels, 102
Epoxy, 101
Sand Lance, 59
Scheck, Art, Art's Shrimp, 80–86
Schmuecker, Tom, 2
Schoolie, 139
Scissors, 4
Sea Pup, 54
Sea trout, flies for
Banded Shrimp, 100
Finesse Fly Silverside, 144
Len's False Pichard, 126
Lil' Hadden, 45
MOG Glass Minnow, 140
the Thing, 122
Utility Minnow, 55
Seducer, Chartreuse & White, 26
See-Through Deceiver, 28
Serviente, Barry, 1
Shirley, Russ, 148
Butt Ugly, 143
Holo Minnow, 143
Rockin' Crabs, 109, 115–117, 124
Shortfin Squid, RM, 87–94
Shrimp (shrimp flies), 79
Art's Shrimp, 80–86
Banded Shrimp, 100
Bonefish Snack, 131
Bugger Shrimp, 102
Cinnamon Cactus
Chenille Shrimp, 105

index

Fuzzy Shrimp, 101
Jumpin' Shrimp, 107
Lenny's Tarpon Shrimp, 107
Mega Shrimp, 105
Mega Shrimp 2, 106
Pearl Imitator Shrimp, 122
Pink Imitator Shrimp, 121
Reggie's Bubble Shrimp, 106
RM Sting, 103
Shrimp Thing, 129
Soda Straw Shrimp, 104
Super Shrimp, 138
Silverside, 46
  Big-Bellied, 56
  Finesse Fly, 144
Silverside Muddler, 48
Simmons, Dexter, 148
  Black Death, 72
  Green Hornet, 72
  Olive Sugarloaf Special, 118
  Rootbeer Sugarloaf Special, 118
Simple flies. See Basic flies
Skipjack, flies for
  JP's Flying Fish, 61
  See-Through Deceiver, 28
Small baitfish flies, 33–61
  Angel Hair Zonker, 47
  Baby Bunker, 46
  Baja Deepdiver, 47
  Bass Magic, 48
  Bay Anchovies, 34–38, 49, 50
  Big-Bellied Silverside, 56
  Boomer, 51
  DJ Hi-Ti, 53
  Enrico's Peanut Bunker, 39–44
  Feather Pup, 54
  Five-Feather Herring, 52
  Glimmer Bunker, 56
  Glimmer Herring, 57
  Glimmer Pinfish, 57
  Gotcha' Clouser, 45
  Green Ghost, 52
  Jail Bait, 55
  JP's Flying Fish, 61
  JP's Mini Mack, 60
  Kris's Bonito Special, 53
  Lil' Hadden, 45

No-Bay-Vy, 58
Rainfish, 58
RM Flatside 2, 51
RM Spitfire, 50
Sea Pup, 54
Silverside, 46
Silverside Muddler, 48
Spearing, 49
Spring Lance, 59
tarpon flies compared with, 63
Tuna Snack, 61
Utility Minnow, 55
Woolly Mullet, 59
Woolly Mummichog, 60
Snapper, flies for
  Banded Shrimp, 100
  JP's Flying Fish, 61
  Pink Imitator Shrimp, 121
  the Thing, 122
Snook, flies for
  Chartreuse & White Seducer, 26
  Everything Fly, 125
  Frank's Roosterfish Fly, 31
  MOG Glass Minnow, 140
  the Nothin' Honey, 29
  Stringbean, 29
  Trashline Squid, 100
  Utility Minnow, 55
Soda Straw Shrimp, 104
Spanish mackerel, flies for
  Finesse Fly Glass Minnow, 144
  Finesse Fly Silverside, 144
  Lil' Hadden, 45
Spearing, 49
Spotted sea trout, the Nothin' Honey for, 29
Spring Lance, 59
Squid (squid flies), 79
  RM Shortfin Squid, 87–94
  Trashline Squid, 100
String, Roy, 145
  Stringbean, 29
Stringbean, 29
Striped bass, flies for
  Bay Anchovy, 34–38
  Deceiver, 27
  Epoxy Sand Eel, 101
  EZ Eel, 95–99
  Finesse Fly Silverside, 144
  Five-Feather Herring, 52

Green Ghost, 52
Ice Cream Cone, 27
Lil' Hadden, 45
MOG Glass Minnow, 140
RM American Eel, 104
RM Flatside 2, 51
RM Shortfin Squid, 87–94
RM Soft Short, 103
RM Sting, 103
Silverside Muddler, 48
squid and eel for, 79
the Whistler, 12–16
Woolly Mullet, 59
Stu Apte Tarpon Fly, 63, 64–66
Stu Apte Tarpon Fly II, 67–71
Sugarloaf Specials
  Olive, 118
  Rootbeer, 118
Super Shrimp, 138
Surf Candies, 133, 134–137
Synthetic materials, 2, 8–9

T

Tan E-Z Crab, 121
Tarpon flies, 63–77
  Black Death, 72
  Black Fly, 77
  Bob's Bread and Butter, 73
  Bob's Tarpon Crab, 73
  Chartreuse & White Seducer, 26
  'Cuda Fly, 17–20
  Everything Fly, 125
  Feather Pup, 54
  Frank's Roosterfish Fly, 31
  Green Hornet, 72
  Green Zima, 74
  hooks for, 6, 7
  Lenny's Tarpon Shrimp, 107
  Len's Tarpon Ocean Runner, 75
  Malzone's Black Death, 76
  Malzone's Blondie, 75
  Malzone's Purple Demon, 76
  the Nothin' Honey, 29
  Pink Imitator Shrimp, 121
  Red Death, 74

Stu Apte Tarpon Fly, 63, 64–66
Stu Apte Tarpon Fly II, 67–71
Tarpon Toy, 77
Trashline Squid, 100
Utility Minnow, 55
Thing, the, 122
  Shrimp, 129
Threads, 7–8
Thunder Creek Minnow, 142
Tiers. See also specific tiers
  featured, 145–148
Tools, 3–5
Trashline Squid, 100
Tuna, flies for
  JP's Flying Fish, 61
  RM Flatside 2, 51
  See-Through Deceiver, 28
  Tuna Snack, 61

U

Ultra Hair, 9, 134
Utility Minnow, 55

V

Veil Fly, 142
Vincelette, Peter
  Albie Candy, 138
  Schoolie, 139
  Super Shrimp, 138
Vises, 3–4

W

Wasicki, Ed, 148
Weakfish, flies for
  Finesse Fly Silverside, 144
  Lil' Hadden, 45
Whip-finishers, 5
Whistler, the, 12–16
White, Jim, 148
  Green Ghost, 52
Wobble Fly, Lenny's Redfish, 141
Woolly Bugger Express, C. H., 30
Woolly Mullet, 59
Woolly Mummichog, 60